EXPLORING SCIENCE

for the
Junior Cycle

STUDENT ACTIVITY BOOK

Michael O'Callaghan
Pat Doyle
Orla Molamphy
Ger Reilly

The Educational Company of Ireland

Tháinig an páipéar a úsáideach sa leabhar seo ó fhoraoisí rialaithe i dtuaisceart na hEorpa. In aghaidh gach crann a leagtar, cuirtear crann amháin eile ar a laghad.

Published 2020
The Educational Company of Ireland
Ballymount Road
Walkinstown
Dublin 12

A member of the Smurfit Kappa Group PLC
© Michael O'Callaghan, Pat Doyle, Orla Molamphy, Ger Reilly

Editor: Life Lines Editorial Services
Design: EMC
Layout: Compuscript
Artwork: Compuscript
Cover Design: EMC

Acknowledgements
Acknowledgement is made to the following for supplying photographs and for permission to reproduce copyright photographs: Science Photo Library, istockphoto, shutterstock.

Acknowledgement is made to the Irish wildlife trust for permission to reproduce material.

Web references in this book are intended as a guide for teachers. At the time of going to press, all web addresses were active and contained information relevant to the topics in this book. However, The Educational Company of Ireland and the authors do not accept responsibility for the views or information contained on these websites. Content and addresses may change beyond our control and pupils should be supervised when investigating websites.

While every care has been taken to trace and acknowledge copyright, the publishers tender their apologies for any accidental infringement where copyright has proved untraceable. They would be pleased to come to a suitable arrangement with the rightful owner in each case.

INTRODUCTION

Welcome to your **Student Activity Book** for *Exploring Science*. Your Student Activity Book works in conjunction with the *Exploring Science* textbook.

Your Student Activity Book contains the following features:

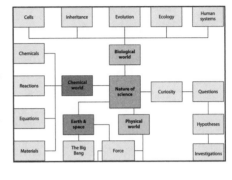

- **Mind Maps**, which you can complete for every chapter, are available through the e-book on www.edcolearning.ie and as printouts from your teacher.

- **Homework questions** are for homework and test whether you have understood the topics covered in each chapter.

  Each question is marked with an icon to signify the level of difficulty:

    ● These are the easiest questions.

    ● These questions are more difficult.

    ● These questions are the most difficult.

- **Activity templates** can be filled in and used as a record of activities you have completed in class.

- **Keywords** questions test your knowledge of the keywords in every chapter.

- **Self-evaluation** sections, at the end of every chapter, have checklists for evaluating how well you felt you understood each topic in a chapter, and provide action plans for filling in what you need to do to improve your learning.

- **Classroom-Based Assessment (CBA) templates**, at the end of your Student Activity Book, can be used when preparing for your CBAs.

- **Features of Quality**, which your teacher will explain to you, show you what is required to enable you to do well in each CBA.

CONTENTS

ACTIVITIES IN THE TEXTBOOK

Homework questions

1 Select the correct term from the box to complete the sentences below.

conclusion   hypothesis   experiment   scientific method

The _scientific method_ is a set of steps scientists follow to answer questions about the world.

A _hypothesis_ is what you think will happen.

An _experiment_ is a test you will carry out to find the answer to a question.

When the experiment is complete, you look at your results, compare with your _hypothesis_ and form a _conclusion_

2 For the following questions, give an example of a possible testable hypothesis.

Question	Possible hypothesis
Is the strength of a bubble affected by adding glycerol to soap and water?	Put a third of glycerol, a third soap and a third water
Is the freezing point of water affected by adding salt?	No it is not.
Is the height of a plant affected by the amount of light it is exposed to?	Yes it is. Depending where you are.

3 Use arrows to match up the word on the left with its correct definition on the right.

Word	Definition
Hypothesis	To gather information about a topic.
Experiment	Information from an experiment that is collected, recorded and analysed.
Independent variable	A possible explanation for something we observe.
Data	Designed to support or contradict a hypothesis.
Research	The one thing that is changed during an experiment.

4 Explain how each of the following laboratory safety rules can reduce the hazard of using an acid.

Laboratory safety rule	Reduces the hazard by...
Wear safety glasses	95%
Wear a lab coat	100%
Wash chemicals off the skin immediately	99.99%
Tie up long hair	100%

Pasteur's investigation

Carrying out investigations and experiments is a key part of how science works. As an example of this we will consider a very famous investigation carried out in the mid-1800s by French scientist Louis Pasteur.

In the 1850s most people (including scientists) believed that living things could be formed from non-living matter. For example, they thought that maggots appearing on rotten meat or fungus growing on bread were examples of living things arising from non-living matter.

Louis Pasteur, a chemist and microbiologist, observed that most living things arose from other living things, for example dogs arose from pups, cats arose from kittens and plants arose from seeds. He (and other scientists) proposed a hypothesis that living things arise from other living things. To test his hypothesis, he designed an experiment that has become famous.

▲ Figure 1.1 *Louis Pasteur*

Pasteur prepared a solution of broth (soup) containing meat and vegetable juices. He poured an equal amount of broth into two flasks. One of the flasks had a long, straight neck; the other had a long, S-shaped curved neck.

He boiled the broth in each flask (which killed any tiny, invisible living things that might have been in the broth) and then left the flasks in a warm room with the necks open to the air.

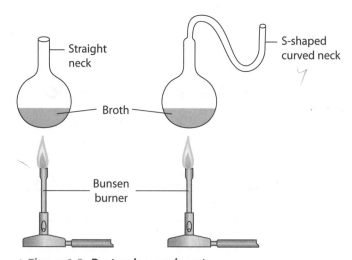

▲ Figure 1.2 *Pasteur's experiment*

After several weeks he observed that the broth in the flask with the straight neck had changed colour and looked cloudy. There was no change in appearance of the broth in the flask with the curved neck.

Pasteur concluded that tiny, invisible particles (he called them 'germs') could pass from the

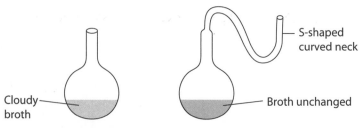

▲ Figure 1.3 *The results of Pasteur's experiment*

outside air down into the straight-necked flask. These germs grew in the broth to produce the cloudy colour. However, the germs were not able to pass through the S-shaped tubing, indicated by the broth in the second flask not changing colour.

Pasteur stated that if life could arise from non-living matter it would be equally likely to arise in both of the flasks. This would result in both flasks turning cloudy. Pasteur concluded that life cannot arise from non-living matter: living things can only arise from living things.

Questions

1 **What observation(s) did Pasteur make that led him to form his hypothesis?**

He poured soup into 2 flaskes one was straight another was S-shaped curved neck.

2 **What was Pasteur's hypothesis?**

That 1 would be the same and the another would changed.

3 **What factors (called fixed or controlled variables) did Pasteur keep the same in the two flasks?**

The amount of broth in flasks.

4 **What factor did Pasteur cause to be different between the two flasks (called the independent variable)?**

He caused the necks to be different

5 **Why did Pasteur set up two flasks in his experiment (i.e. why is a control important in science experiments)?** *To see which one would change quicker.*

6 **Why was it necessary to boil the broth in each flask?** *To see how the smoke went out differently.*

7 **Did Pasteur's experiment support or contradict his hypothesis?** *No it did not.*

8 **What, do you think, might have happened if he had sealed each flask after boiling the broths?** *The smoke would be trapped.*

9 **Pasteurisation is a process that was first proposed by Louis Pasteur. Research the process of pasteurisation and answer the following questions.**

(a) **What is meant by 'pasteurisation'?** *A partial sterilize of a product.*

(b) Give two examples of materials that can be pasteurised.

(i) Milk

(ii) Wine

(c) Why do pasteurised products remain fresh for longer than non-pasteurised products?

Pasteurised products reduce

(d) Why do pasteurised products decay or spoil after some time?

They're kept in a fridge

10 Keywords. Write one short sentence using each of the following words:

(a) Prediction What you think will happen

(b) Hypothesis When a prediction is tested

(c) Experiment When carrying out a hypothesis

(d) Independent variable Where one thing is changed

(e) Dependent variable Which is the factor that changes as a result of our investigation

(f) Controlled variable where all other factors are the same.

(g) Quantitative data Where the data involves the use of numbers

(h) Qualitative data Which describes something without the use of numbers.

(i) Accuracy How accurate something is

(j) Precision the quality condition or fact of being exact and accurate.

(k) Conclusion The answer.

Understanding scientific communications

Read the following two articles and then answer the questions on them.

Article 1

Is recycling worthwhile?

The short answer is: Yes.

Recycling is a process where materials from waste products such as paper, glass, plastic or metals may be used to make other products instead of throwing them away. Recycling is important in today's world if we want to protect this planet for future generations. When we convert old and waste products into new products we are saving resources and sending less rubbish to landfill sites, which helps to reduce soil, water and air pollution.

Aluminium from scrap

Recycling helps to conserve important raw materials such as aluminium. In 2010 the worldwide production of aluminium was 41.4 million tonnes, and more than 3% of the world's entire electrical supply went to extract this metal. Aluminium recycling is the melting of scrap metal, which is far less expensive and energy intensive than creating new aluminium. This is the reason why 31% of all aluminium in the United States of America comes from recycled scrap.

Methane from landfill

In 2013 methane accounted for about 10% of US greenhouse gas emissions from human activities. Methane traps more radiation than carbon dioxide, and its impact on climate change due to global warming is twenty-five times greater than CO_2 over a hundred-year period. The United States EPA (Environmental Protection Agency) has identified landfill sites as the greatest source of methane emissions and the decomposition of paper as the biggest contributor; so the more paper that is recycled, the less methane that is released. This also reduces the number of trees that are cut down each year, which in turn helps our environment because trees help to absorb carbon dioxide from the air.

Recycling – it's the responsibility of all of us

Recycling reduces the demand for energy. Recycling just one aluminium can saves energy equivalent to running a TV for three hours. Imagine that ratio for millions of cans! So far, Europe has led the way in recycling packaging materials.

This is due to the Packaging and Packaging Waste Directive of 1994, which calls for all manufacturers and retailers to share the recycling burden. Higher hygiene standards, smaller households and the rise in the consumption of ready-made meals have all contributed to an increase in packaging waste, so it is very important that we all pay attention to the items we buy and to the quantity and type of materials used for the packaging. We are all responsible for the care of our planet. It is up to each one of us to be stewards of our environment and recycling is one way in which we can be active in caring for and maintaining it.

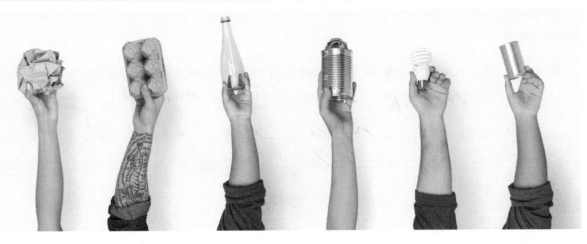

Article 2

Is recycling good for our environment?

Samantha MacBride, author of *Recycling Reconsidered* states: 'Recycling is what it is, but it's not saving the Earth.'

In America in 2010, 85 million tons of waste were diverted from landfill sites to be recycled or composted. This is the same as removing the emissions of 36 million passenger cars. Although this is a huge amount, on the other side of the balance it is important to realise the cost and efficiency of recycling.

Is recycling cost effective?

Recycling may not always be cost effective as there is a need to build large factories to process the waste. The recycling process may create more pollution problems as the waste undergoes cleaning, storage and transportation. For example, in waste-paper processing plants the reclaimed pulp requires

bleaching before use and the concentrations of chlorine required can be a toxic hazard and a pollutant if not handled properly.

Do recycled products last for long?

Most recycled items are made from waste that tends to be fragile and may last for only a short time. Aluminium may be recycled a number of times with no loss of quality, but plastics are generally recycled for one use only, e.g. plastic fibres used for insulation, carpets or clothing. So when you choose a recycled plastic product, it may seem like a good idea to help try to save the environment, but in some cases you may be just delaying not preventing its eventual trip to the landfill site.

Waste causing waste

Recycling sites are not safe places. Large amounts of waste are dumped and this may lead to the spread of diseases, which may be harmful to the people who are working at the sites and handling the waste. Sometimes waste is mixed with water during the recycling process and this may lead to toxins in the waste water, which in turn may affect drinking water. For example, the printing inks on paper may contain lead, zinc and chromium and the process to remove the ink could cause the metals to enter the water stream. Electronic devices contain many valuable and rare compounds. Recycling them may involve the devices being

transported around the world, thus using vast amounts of energy.

The future of waste

Recycling often occurs on a small scale, such as in homes or schools, but not so much on a larger scale, such as in industries. Only 15% of New York city's municipal waste is diverted from landfills, but new programmes are being implemented in the city to bring up the rate to 30% by 2017, saving the city $60 million annually. When weighing the pros and cons of recycling, it is important to realise that the cost and efficiency of recycling varies from material to material. Maybe it would make more sense to reduce consumption altogether, as well as improve the initial product design.

Questions

1 **What are the advantages and disadvantages of recycling, as discussed in the articles?**

An Advantage is if we recycle then the planet will be here for longer. A disadvantage if we don't recycle we're damaging the ozone layer

2 Do you think that recycling is helping to save our environment? Explain why you think that.

Yes. It's because we are reusing our materials and less damage to the ozone layer.

3 What do you think Samantha MacBride means by 'Recycling is what it is, but it's not saving the Earth'?

I think she means that if we recycle more fossil fuels are going in the air.

4 Do you think the efficiency of recycling varies from material to material? Explain why you think that.

No. I think it only works for some specific materials because some materials won't cope.

5 What is your opinion on whether recycling is having a negative or positive impact on our environment?

If it is having a negative impact then people can't do anything. A positive one the whole world can do something to save it.

6 Recycling is important, but what two other things would help reduce the amount of waste going to landfill or recycling plants?

(i) Don't litter

(ii) Don't waste food

7 The article gives figures for the United States. Find out how much waste goes to landfill and is diverted from landfill in Ireland. Make sure you say for which year your figures relate.

85 million tons are diverted.

8 The first article mentions the US EPA.

(a) What does 'EPA' stand for?

Environmental protection agency

(b) Does Ireland have an EPA? If so, what is its website address?

No. It does not have a EPA.

Read the following article and then answer the questions that follow.

Planet Earth

Our planet, Earth, can support life. This happens because the Sun is near enough to keep Earth warm, but not so close that Earth does not freeze. There have been many times through the history of Earth when very cold periods occurred (these are known as the ice ages) and many times when Earth was very warm. Earth is warming again, but why does the current warming of our planet worry us so much?

Natural or not?

The changes in climate that took place before the 1900s were due to natural changes in Earth's climate. Our current climate change is as a direct result of what people are doing. In addition, this current climate change is happening at a much faster rate than before and is affecting a lot more areas on the planet. So what took place in our history that has led to this accelerated warming of Earth? Around two hundred years ago the Industrial Revolution took place. This was a time of great change in manufacturing and technology. All of these changes required power and electricity. The energy used to supply the power came from the burning of fossil fuels: coal, oil and gas. The burning of these fuels released vast quantities of carbon dioxide gas into our atmosphere.

The greenhouse effect

Some carbon dioxide gas exists in our atmosphere naturally. It acts like a blanket, trapping heat energy within our atmosphere, which allows Earth to have a warm enough temperature to support life. This warming is called the greenhouse effect. But the additional burning of the fossil fuels that has been taking place since the Industrial Revolution has dramatically increased that warming greenhouse effect. This has resulted in Earth experiencing a greater rate of change in its climate and in its temperature than at any other time in Earth's history.

How do we know climate change is taking place?

How can we observe that climate change is taking place? Unfortunately, there are far too many effects that we can see: flooding, droughts, melting of polar ice sheets, shrinking glaciers, and rising sea levels. In addition, the warmer the planet gets, the more water that evaporates. This has resulted in more violent storms occurring at much greater frequency, and warming waters dissolving more carbon dioxide, making oceans more acidic. This list makes for compelling evidence that this is not just another natural warm cycle, but rather a human made problem.

We need more trees!

In addition to burning fossil fuels, humans have also made other choices that have accelerated the effect of carbon dioxide gas. Trees take in carbon dioxide gas as part of photosynthesis, to enable the plant to make food. This helps us by removing carbon dioxide from the atmosphere. Again humans have made a major impact as we have cut down, cleared away and removed enormous areas of rainforest, which contain the bulk of Earth's supply of trees.

This process is called deforestation. It is this process that has a direct link to our climate change problem – the fewer trees that are available to take in carbon dioxide gas, the more of this gas remains in the atmosphere.

Denying it doesn't change it

Even with all the evidence that is available to us that links climate change directly to human impact, there are many people who believe that climate change is nothing to panic about. In fact, some people believe that there may be a conspiracy here, and that this whole climate change issue is being greatly exaggerated.

There are groups within our society that think the current level of carbon dioxide concentration in the atmosphere is an appropriate level. Other groups think that the alarm over climate change has created opportunities for companies and agencies to get funding to develop new forms of energy and to develop means by which to reduce the effect of climate change.

The opposing arguments are also compelling.

The people who oppose climate change have accepted that scientific evidence does show that changes in our climate have taken place but that these changes are not necessarily directly as a result of human activity; that the changes in fact are just another natural warming cycle of Earth.

Whichever way we look at this, for or against the arguments relating to climate change, the key fact is that Earth is warming at its greatest rate since records began. We now have to approach this problem and try to solve it, no matter what argument we believe. The underlying fact is that we all need to solve and fix this issue, regardless of who or what we think is causing it to take place.

Questions

1 **What evidence does this article state to show that climate change is taking place?**

It shows that every place are creating fossil fuels and that carbondioxide is more of the problem

2 **Which three substances are known as fossil fuels?**

(i) *coal*

(ii) *oil*

(iii) *gas*

3 **Which gas is the main cause of climate change?**

It is carbondioxide is the main cause.

4 **Where does this gas come from?**

It is there naturally and comes from excretion

5 **What is happening on Earth to show that climate change is taking place?**

There are more floods, droughts and melting polar ice.

6 **What does the word 'conspiracy' mean? (Look it up in a dictionary, if you need to.)**

It is a secret plan by a group to do something unlawful or harmful.

7 What arguments are put forward in the article to suggest that climate change is a conspiracy?

People still think climate change is nothing.

8 Do you think climate change is taking place? Why do you think this?

Yes because the polar ice is melting the ocean is rising.

9 Do you think deforestation has a direct link to climate change? Why do you think this?

Yes. It is a direct link.

Mind maps

Mind maps are a useful learning aid. They are a visual way of grouping ideas and facts and reminding you of associations. You add only the briefest of information but the mind map can give you an overview of a large topic and acts as a reminder of the different elements of that topic.

The mind map included in this chapter attempts to show that the nature of science is central to all four sections of science (biological world, chemical world, physical world and Earth and space).

The nature of science is summarised by the pathway starting with curiosity, questions, hypotheses, etc.

Each of the four sections then emerges from the nature of science. Each section has a pathway that describes the main topics contained within the section. For example, the physical world contains chapters on force, motion, measurement, energy and electricity.

Note that many of the topics covered may apply to more than one section of the course. This is shown by the links from force to the physical world, the universe and to Earth and space.

Mind maps for all other chapters in this Activity Book are available on **www.edcolearning.ie**

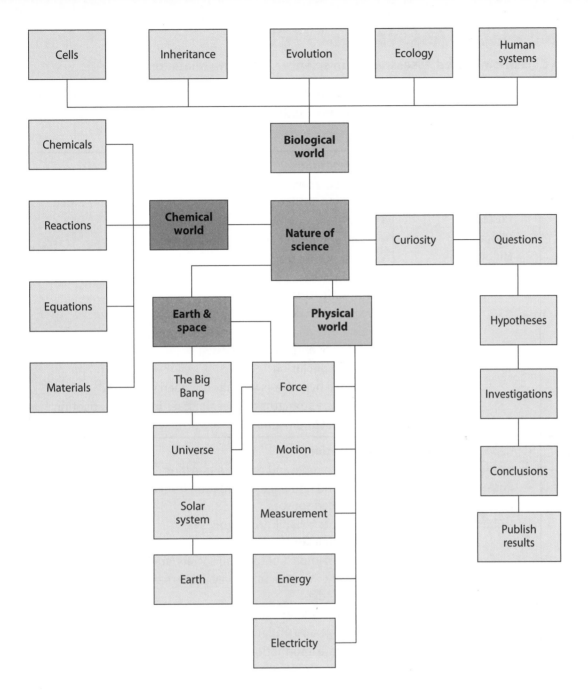

Self evaluation – The nature of science

Now that you have completed this chapter, how well do you feel you understand each of the following (tick the relevant column)?

Topic	🙂	😐	🙁
The nature of science		✓	
Keywords	✓	✓	
Understanding scientific communications	✓		
Mind maps		✓	

Action plan: What I need to do to improve my learning _____

_____

Classroom-Based Assessments (CBAs)

There are two Classroom-Based Assessments in science. They both relate to:

Priorities for learning and teaching such as **investigating** and **communicating** in science, while at the same time developing a **knowledge** and **understanding** of science, which are vital to working like a scientist.

Extended Experimental Investigation (EEI)	• Report (400–600 words excluding tables, graphs, etc.) • Posters • Podcasts • Multimedia	**Investigation:** • Decide question • Form hypothesis • Consider variables, reliability and fairness • Use equipment correctly and safely • Describe method • Record data **Communication:** • Present data • Describe relationship between variables **Knowledge and understanding:** • Draw conclusion • State if hypothesis has/has not been supported • Describe strengths and weaknesses in the investigation • Suggest improvements
Science in society (SSI)	• Report (650–800 words) • Posters • Podcasts • Multimedia	**Investigation:** • Choose topic and research question • Find and reference information from a number of balanced sources • Evaluate reliability of sources **Communication:** • Explain impact of topic on society/environment • Present in a structured way using relevant scientific knowledge • Explain different sides of the argument **Knowledge and understanding:** • Evaluate information • Link information to the topic • Review information using scientific explanations • Give justified explanations

Ideas for EEI (CB1)

Is heat a factor that affects the solubility of carbon dioxide in fizzy drinks?

Does the colour of light affect the growth of a plant?

Is the performance of a solar cell affected by dust or sand particles on its surface?

Ideas for SSI (CBA2)

Will global warming make tropical diseases such as malaria travel to northern Europe – including Ireland?

Can brain stimulation cure mental illness?

Does eating antioxidants really help to prevent cancer or other diseases?

Is fracking causing earthquakes and other environmental problems?

CHAPTER 2

LIVING THINGS AND CELLS

📄 Log onto www.edcolearning.ie to find the **Mind Map** for this chapter.

Homework questions

1 Tick (✓) the correct column to say whether each of the following features is true for a plant cell, an animal cell or both:

Feature of cells	True for plant cell	True for animal cell	True for both
(a) Has a cell wall	✓		
(b) Never has chlorophyll		✓	
(c) Has a nucleus			✓
(d) Has a cell membrane			✓
(e) Has a vacuole			✓
(f) Has DNA			✓

2 (a) A microscope has an eyepiece lens that is marked ×20. What does this mean?

It increases the viewing sight by ×20

(b) If the same microscope has an objective lens marked ×10, what is the total magnification when using these two lenses?

× 30

(c) If you were using this microscope and you wanted a total magnification of 400, what magnification would the objective lens have to be?

× 40?

3 Write the correct cell part from the words below to match with the correct statement. The first one has been completed for you.

cell membrane   cell wall   ~~chloroplasts~~   nucleus   vacuole   cytoplasm   mitochondrion

Statement	Part of cell
Green structures in plant cells that carry out photosynthesis	chloroplasts
Is made of cellulose	Vacuole
Supplies the cell with energy	Mitochondrion
Controls the activities in the cell	Nucleus
Controls what passes in and out of the cell	Cell membrane
Makes plant cells strong	Cell wall
Is the liquid in a cell around the nucleus	Cytoplasm

LIVING THINGS AND CELLS   13

4 Plant cells have cell walls but animal cells do not.

(a) What problem might a plant have if its cells did not have walls?

They would no longer have a structure

(b) Why do animal cells not need walls?

Animal cells

5 (a) When using a microscope a light source passes up through the stage. Why is the light source needed?

A light source is needed to give the viewer
a better view of the structure

(b) Why can you view only thin structures under a microscope?

Thicker structures require a lot more
light and magnification than thinner structures.

(c) Why are animal and plant cells stained before being viewed under the microscope?

A stain is added to the cell to
show each and every feature of the cell.

6 Anton van Leeuwenhoek is often called 'the father of microscopy'.

(a) Find out why he first started using microscopes and where he got his microscopes or lenses.

_____

_____

(b) He described seeing what he called 'animalcules'. Find out what animalcules are now called.

_____

_____

7 Another famous scientist was called 'the English father of microscopy'. He was the first person to use the word 'cell'.

(a) Find out who this scientist was.

_____

_____

(b) What was he looking at when he first used the word 'cell', and why did he use this word?

_____

_____

8   Circle the living objects in the diagram below:

Ania

9   The diagram below represents an instrument that is used to examine cells.

(a)   What name is given to this instrument? _microscope_

(b)   The parts labelled A and B have the same function. What is this function?
to give a the view of the structure

(c)   Name the part labelled C. _stage_

(d)   The diagram shows a plant cell. Name the parts of the plant cell labelled X and Y.
Cell wall & Nucleus

10   A student prepared a slide of cheek cells.

(a)   Name a stain the student should use to see the cheek cells more clearly.
Iodine

(b)   The diagram on the right shows a cheek cell.

(i)   Name the parts of the cell labelled A, B and C.
Cell membrane, Cytoplasm, Nucleus

(ii)   What important structures are located in part B?
Mitochondrian

(iii)   Name one substance that might pass into the cell through the structure labelled A.
Oxygen.

11 Keywords. Write one short sentence using each of the following words:

(a) Organism _a living thing_

(b) Vertebrate _Animals with backbones_

(c) Invertebrate _Animals without backbones._

(d) Biodiversity _____

(e) Cell _The basic building blocks of life._

(f) Nutrition _The way an organism gets its food_

(g) Excretion _The way an organism gets rid of its waste_

(h) Response _The way an organism reacts to its surroundings_

(i) Reproduction _When living things produced new living things._

(j) Cell membrane _This allows things to move in + out of the cell._

(k) Nucleus _Controls all the activity in the cell_

(l) Vacuole _Storage departments of liquids._

(m) Mitochondrion _Powerhouse of the cell._

(n) Chloroplasts _____ in the ___ contained chlorophyll used in photosynthesis._

Activity 2.1: How can we examine animal cells?

(a) Date on which you carried out this activity _____

(b) In this activity what type of animal cell did you look at? _____

(c) What stain did you use? _____

(d) Why did you use a stain? _____

_____

(e) What safety features did you consider and what did you do to reduce the risks?

_____

_____

Record your results.

At low-power magnification

(f) What magnification was the eyepiece lens you used?

_____

(g) What magnification was the low-power objective lens that you used?

_____

(h) What was the total low-power magnification that you used?

_____

(i)   Which focus wheel did you use? _____

_____

(j)   In the circle draw a diagram of about ten of the cells
       that you saw under low power.

At high-power magnification

(k)   What magnification was the eyepiece lens you used?

_____

(l)   What magnification was the high-power objective
       lens that you used? _____

(m)   What was the total high-power magnification that you
       used? _____

(n)   Which focus wheel did you use? _____

_____

(o)   In the circle draw a diagram of a single cell that you
       saw under high power and label the three main parts.

Observe the cheek cells for features such as:

(p)   Are they all the same shape? _____

(q)   Are they all the same size? _____

(r)   What colour is the cytoplasm? _____

(s)   What colour is the nucleus? _____

(t)   Can you see any particles in the cytoplasm? _____

(u)   What conclusion did you reach at the end of activity 2.1?

_____

_____

_____

✎ Activity 2.2:   How can we examine plant cells?

(a)   Date on which you carried out this activity _____

(b)   In this activity what type of plant cell did you look at? _____

(c)   What stain did you use? _____

(d)   What colour was the nucleus when using the stain? _____

(e)   What differences did you notice between the plant cell and the animal cell from the
       previous activity? _____

_____

Record your results.

At low-power magnification

(f)   What magnification was the eyepiece lens you used?

_____

(g)   What magnification was the low-power objective lens that you used?

_____

(h)   What was the total low-power magnification that you used? _____

(i)   Which focus wheel did you use? _____

_____

(j)   In the circle draw a diagram of about ten of the cells that you saw under low power.

At high-power magnification

(k)   What magnification was the eyepiece lens you used?

_____

(l)   What magnification was the high-power objective lens that you used? _____

(m)   What was the total high-power magnification that you used? _____

(n)   Which focus wheel did you use? _____

_____

(o)   In the circle draw a diagram of a single cell that you saw under high power and label the main parts.

Reflection

(p)   What are two things you liked about this activity?

•   _____

•   _____

(q)   What did you find difficult about this activity?

_____

(r)   If you were to do this activity again, what would you do differently?

_____

Self evaluation – Living things and cells

Now that you have completed this chapter, how well do you feel you understand each of the following (tick the relevant column)?

Topic	😊	😐	☹️
The differences between living and non-living things			
The different groups of living things			
The differences between vertebrates and invertebrates			
What cell membranes are and what they do			
What the nucleus is and what it does			
What the cytoplasm is and where it is in a cell			
What a cell wall is and what it does			
What a vacuole is and what it does			
The differences between animal and plant cells			
The names of the parts of a microscope			
How to use a microscope			

Action plan: **What I need to do to improve my learning** _____

_____

_____

_____

_____

_____

PASSING ON CHARACTERISTICS

Log onto **www.edcolearning.ie** to find the **Mind Map** for this chapter.

Homework questions

1   Tick the relevant box for whether each of the following statements is true or false:

		True	False
(a)	Asexual reproduction involves only one parent.	☑	☐
(b)	Gametes are needed for sexual reproduction.	☑	☐
(c)	The offspring from asexual reproduction have different genes.	☐	☑
(d)	Some variations are learned during life.	☑	☐
(e)	Genes are bigger than chromosomes.	☑	☐
(f)	Chromosomes are found in the cytoplasm of cells.	☐	☑
(g)	A dominant version of a gene prevents the recessive version from working.	☑	☐
(h)	A cell normally contains three copies of each gene.	☐	☑
(i)	Each gamete contains half the number of genes compared to the parent cell.	☑	☐

2   The gene for hair colour in humans has two versions. The dominant version (B) causes brown hair and the non-dominant, or recessive, version (b) produces red hair. John has the combination Bb and Alice has the combination bb.

(a)   What colour hair does John have?

Brown hair

(b)   What colour hair does Alice have?

Red hair

	B	b
b	Bb	bb
b	bb	bb

(c)   What versions of the gene might John's gametes contain?

Dominant version

(d)   What versions of the gene might Alice's gametes contain?

Recessive version

(e)   What genetic combinations might their offspring have?

_Bb, bb_

(f)   What is the percentage probability that one of their children might have brown hair?

_50%_

3 (a) Dark-coloured hair (D) is dominant over red hair (d). If both parents have dark hair, show how they could have a red-haired child.

Parents' genes ___Dd___ and ___Dd___

Gametes ___Dark___ and ___red___

Offspring hair colour ___dark___ and ___red___ and ___dark___ and ___red___

(b) What is the percentage chance that they will not have a red-haired child? ___50%___

4 List of characteristics:

having freckles	riding a bicycle	tying a knot	blue eyes

(a) Give one example of an inherited human characteristic from the list above.

___having freckles___

(b) Give one example of a non-inherited (or acquired) human characteristic from the list above.

___riding a bike___

(c) What structures, contained on chromosomes, are responsible for inherited characteristics?

___

5 Separate the following into inherited and non-inherited characteristics (tick the correct column in the table).

Characteristic	Inherited	Non-inherited
Gelled hair		✓
Long nails		✓
A scar		✓
Brown eyes	✓	
A wide smile	✓	
Five toes	✓	
A body piercing		✓
Shape of the earlobes	✓	
Speaking a language		✓
Being able to subtract		✓
Large eyes	✓	
Ability to play the piano		✓

6 In rats, a dark coat (D) is dominant over light coat (d). Carry out the following genetic crosses and predict the ratio of dark-coated and light-coated rats that could be formed in each cross.

(a) Parents are DD and dd
Gametes are __dark__ and __red__
Offspring genes are __Dd__
Offspring coat colour is __dark__
Ratio (%) of dark-coated and light-coated offspring is __100%__

(b) Parents are DD and Dd
Gametes are _____ and _____
Offspring genes are _____ and _____
Offspring coat colours are _____ and _____
Ratio (%) of dark-coated and light-coated offspring is _____

(c) Parents are Dd and dd
Gametes are _____ and _____
Offspring genes are _____ and _____
Offspring coat colours are _____ and _____
Ratio (%) of dark-coated and light-coated offspring is _____

(d) Parents are Dd and Dd
Gametes are _____ and _____
Offspring genes are _____ and _____ and _____ and _____
Offspring coat colours are _____ and _____ and _____ and _____
Ratio (%) of dark-coated and light-coated offspring is _____

7 Keywords. Write one short sentence using each of the following words:

(a) Asexual reproduction _The formation of a new organism containing ↓ parent only_

(b) Sexual reproduction _The formation of a new organism with 2 parents_

(c) Gamete _A sex cell_

(d) Zygote _Fusion of 2 gametes_

(e) Fertilisation _____

(f) Characteristics _Inherited genes_

(g) Variation _____

(h) DNA _____

(i) Dominant _Expressed as a trait_

(j) Recessive _____

(k) Genes _____

(l) Chromosomes _____

8 Phenylketonuria (PKU) is a genetic disorder. It is caused by a person having two recessive versions of a gene (pp). If the person has at least one dominant version of the gene they are normal.

PKU means the person cannot break down a chemical from their diet. This leads to major health problems. Fortunately, PKU can be detected in a blood sample taken from a baby soon after birth. If the baby has PKU they must avoid eating the chemical for the rest of their life.

The following pedigree analysis represents a family, some of whom have PKU. The square symbols represent males and the round symbols represent females.

In addition, the shaded symbols represent people with PKU and the clear symbols represent people without the disorder.

(a) How many children did couple 1 and 2 have? _____

(b) How many girls did couple 1 and 2 have? _____

(c) What was the genetic combination or genotype of all the shaded people? _____

(d) What was the genotype of person 1? _____

(e) How many boys did couple 6 and 7 have? _____

(f) What was the chance that person 9 had PKU? _____

(g) How many granddaughters did couple 1 and 2 have? _____

Activity 3.1: How can we investigate some inherited traits?

(a) Date on which you carried out this activity _____

(b) Record your results in the table below.

Trait	Individual results	Class result totals
Attached ear lobes		
Detached ear lobes		
Tongue roller		
Not a tongue roller		
Dimples		
No dimples		
Left-handed		
Right-handed		
Freckles		
No freckles		

Trait	Individual results	Class result totals
Curly hair		
Straight hair		
Left thumb on top		
Right thumb on top		
Pointed hairline		
Straight hairline		

(c) Of the pairs of traits investigated:

(i) Which trait was the most common? _____

(ii) Which trait was closest to a 50:50 ratio? _____

Reflection

(d) What are two things you liked about this activity?

• _____

• _____

(e) What did you find difficult about this activity?

_____

(f) If you were to do this activity again, what would you do differently?

_____

Self evaluation – Passing on characteristics

Now that you have completed this chapter, how well do you feel you understand each of the following (tick the relevant column)?

Topic	🙂	😐	🙁
Asexual reproduction			
Sexual reproduction			
Examples of genetic or inherited characteristics			
Examples of non-inherited characteristics			
Chromosomes			
Genetic crosses			

Action plan: What I need to do to improve my learning _____

_____

THE ORIGINS OF LIVING THINGS

Log onto **www.edcolearning.ie** to find the **Mind Map** for this chapter.

Homework questions

1 Tick the inherited traits from the following list:

Red hair ☐   Suntan ☐   Speaking a language ☐

Long hair ☐   Eye colour ☐   Having two lungs ☐

Freckles ☐   Need for spectacles ☐

2 Who is the scientist most closely associated with the theory of evolution?

_____

3 The following is a summary of the theory of evolution by natural selection. Write out the summary and insert the correct words from the following list to complete the summary.

genes	survive	adapted	mutated	competition	extinct

More organisms are produced than can _____ due to a lack of resources. This means that organisms struggle for the resources needed to survive. This causes _____ for scarce resources. Within a group of the same species some of the organisms are different due to _____ genes. Those organisms that are better _____ to their environment will survive and reproduce. As a result they pass on their _____ to the next generation. Those organisms that are less well adapted reproduce less often and die. This causes the species to become _____.

4 Alfred Russel Wallace is also associated with discovering the theory of evolution.

(a) Write a short account of his life. (Write your account here or type it up and paste the printout here.)

_____

_____

_____

_____

_____

_____

(b) Explain why Wallace is not as well-known as Charles Darwin even though both of them had similar ideas around the same period of time.

_____

_____

_____

5 Why are dogs and cats considered to be different species?

_____

6 Natural selection allows those organisms that are most suited to their environment to survive and to pass on their genes. Suggest why the following organisms might be suited to their environment:

(a) Hawks with good eyesight

_____

(b) Frogs that have coloration to allow them to blend in with vegetation

_____

(c) Animals that produce a thicker coat of fur or wool in winter

_____

(d) Plants that have thorns

_____

7 The table below describes four female rabbits living on a beach with light brown sand. There are many plants close to the beach.

Description of each rabbit	Colour of fur			
	White	Brown	Black	Black and brown
Running speed	6 m/sec	7 m/sec	10 m/sec	8 m/sec
Number of offspring	3	14	0	6
Lifespan	6 months	4 years	2 years	1 year

(a) From the information provided in the table, which rabbit is most suited to its environment? Explain how this rabbit is so well adapted.

_____

_____

(b) Suggest one reason why the white rabbit has such a short lifespan.

_____

(c) Why might running speed affect the lifespan of a rabbit?

_____

(d) Consider the information in the table and predict which type of rabbit is most likely to survive in this environment.

_____

8 Bacteria are killed by antibiotics. From time to time a bacterium becomes resistant to an antibiotic and is no longer killed by it. As most of the other bacteria are killed the new bacterium can multiply and grow very rapidly.

This process has occurred many times over the last 50 years or so. As a result, there are now groups of bacteria (such as MRSA) that are resistant to almost all antibiotics. These are called multi-resistant bacteria. The development of antibiotic-resistant bacteria is an example of evolution over a very short period of time.

(a) Use your knowledge of the theory of evolution to explain how a bacterium might develop resistance to an antibiotic.

_____

_____

(b) What is the danger of multi-resistant bacteria?

_____

_____

(c) In societies where antibiotics are not used, multi-resistant bacteria have not evolved. Find out why this is the case.

_____

_____

9 Why humans store fat

It is believed that the first humans arose in Africa (between one million and 200 000 years ago). For many of these humans, food was scarce at certain times of the year. Those humans who did not have the gene to convert carbohydrates to fat remained thin. However, they often starved when food was scarce (such as during severe water shortages).

At some time in the past it is thought that some of our ancestors developed a gene to enable them to store fat. This allowed them to survive harsh conditions. When they reproduced they passed this gene on to the next generation. In time those humans who could not store fat became extinct. Those who could store fat gave rise to modern humans.

(a) Why might food have been scarce at certain times of the year in Africa?

_____

(b) Suggest a disadvantage of not being able to store fat.

_____

(c) How might the gene to allow fat storage have first arisen?

_____

(d) What was the advantage for our ancestors of storing fat?

_____

(e) In terms of diet and activity levels why is the fat storage gene now causing so many problems?

_____

_____

10 Wild foxes are naturally inclined to avoid humans and are often aggressive. In recent years Russian scientists bred a number of foxes in captivity. From each litter of fox cubs born they selected the tamest foxes. They bred the tamest fox cubs together and repeated this process with each generation of cubs born.

After a number of generations they found that all the fox cubs born were tame and friendly around humans. They behaved just like tame dogs.

(a) Suggest why wild foxes might want to avoid humans.

_____

_____

(b) Why did tame foxes develop so rapidly in this experiment?

_____

_____

(c) The new tame foxes cannot be released into the wild. Why, do you think, this is the case?

_____

_____

11 The mountain hare is found in northern European countries. In the high mountains, its coat colour changes from brown in summer to a white coat in winter. The picture shows the mountain hare moulting (losing its white coat) in early spring.

(a) What is the benefit to the mountain hare of having a brown coat in summer?

_____

_____

(b) Why might the coat turn white in winter in the high mountains?

_____

_____

(c) If a hare failed to moult in spring it would remain white in summer. What might happen to such a hare?

_____

_____

(d) Irish hares rarely turn white. Why is this, do you think?

_____

_____

12 Keywords. Write one short sentence using each of the following words:

(a) Biodiversity _____

(b) Fossil _____

(c) Extinct _____

(d) Species _____

(e) Natural selection _____

(f) Mutation _____

(g) Evolution _____

(h) Adaptation _____

Self evaluation – The origins of living things

Now that you have completed this chapter, how well do you feel you understand each of the following (tick the relevant column)?

Topic	☺	😐	☹
Biodiversity			
Species			
Mutations			
Living things produce huge numbers of offspring			
The environment supports only some living things			
The struggle for existence			
Inherited variations			
Natural selection			
The diversity of life arises from evolution			

Action plan: What I need to do to improve my learning _____

_____

_____

_____

_____

CHAPTER 5
THE PATH OF FOOD

Log onto **www.edcolearning.ie** to find the **Mind Map** for this chapter.

Homework questions

1   Name the part of the digestive system found between each of the following:

   (a)   The mouth and the stomach

   _____

   (b)   The stomach and the large intestine

   _____

   (c)   The oesophagus and the small intestine

   _____

2   Write the parts of the digestive system named in column A in the correct order in column B.

Column A	Column B
Rectum	
Stomach	
Mouth	
Anus	
Small intestine	
Oesophagus	
Large intestine	

3   On the diagram to the right:

   (a)   Mark the location of each of the following:
         oesophagus
         stomach
         liver
         pancreas

   (b)   Mark with the letter D the location where most digestion takes place.

   (c)   Mark with the letter A the location where most absorption takes place.

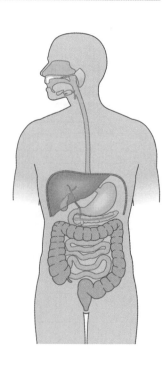

4 Select the correct word from the list to answer each of the following questions.

liver   enzymes   digestion   amylase   canine   peristalsis

(a)   The breakdown of food is called _____.

(b)   The type of teeth found between the incisors and the premolars are called _____ teeth.

(c)   Chemical digestion requires _____.

(d)   _____ is an example of an enzyme.

(e)   Food is pushed through the intestines by _____.

(f)   Bile is produced in the _____.

5 Rewrite the functions from column B into column C to match the structures in column A.

A	B	C
Molar teeth	Contains hydrochloric acid	
Rectum	Chew and grind food	
Large intestine	Absorbs food	
Stomach	Stores faeces	
Small intestine	Reabsorbs water	

6 What is the difference between physical and chemical digestion?

_____

_____

7 Fill in the following table to show what high-fibre foods you like (or eat) and some that you don't like (or eat).

High-fibre foods I like (or eat)	High-fibre foods I do not like (or eat)

8 What, do you think, would be the main problem for each of the following?

(a)   A person who has no teeth

_____

_____

(b)   A person with too much acid in their stomach

_____

_____

(c)   A person with too little acid in their stomach

_____

_____

(d)   A person who is missing the first part of their small intestine

_____

_____

(e)   A person who is missing the second part of their small intestine

_____

_____

(f)   A person who is missing their large intestine

_____

_____

9   (a)   Name an enzyme in the digestive system.

_____

(b)   State the substance this enzyme acts on.

_____

(c)   What product is formed by the action of this enzyme?

_____

10   If food passes too slowly through our intestines we may suffer from constipation.

(a)   In what part of the intestines is water reabsorbed?

_____

(b)   How does constipation relate to the reabsorption of water in the intestines?

_____

_____

(c)   How can we alter our diet to prevent constipation?

_____

_____

11   (a)   Why do dogs have such large canine teeth?

_____

_____

(b) Why do rabbits have such large incisor teeth?

_____

_____

(c) People who do not chew their food properly may suffer from indigestion. Suggest why this may be the case.

_____

_____

12 Imagine you are a piece of food. Write an account of what happens to you as you pass through the digestive system from the mouth to the anus.

_____

_____

_____

_____

_____

13 The graph shows the time taken for 1 gram of starch to be fully digested at different temperatures.

(a) Name the enzyme that digests starch.

_____

(b) Name one place in the digestive system where starch is digested.

_____

(c) At what temperature was the starch digested:

(i) Most quickly? _____

(ii) Most slowly? _____

(d) At what temperatures did it take 5 minutes for the starch to be digested?

_____

14 Keywords. Write one short sentence using each of the following words:

(a) Physical digestion

_____

(b) Chemical digestion

_____

(c) Catalyst

_____

(d) Amylase

_____

(e) Oesophagus

_____

(f) Peristalsis

_____

(g) Small intestine

_____

(h) Bile

_____

(i) Egestion

_____

Self evaluation – The path of food

Now that you have completed this chapter, how well do you feel you understand each of the following (tick the relevant column)?

Topic	😊	😐	☹
Physical digestion			
Chemical digestion			
Teeth			
Enzymes			
Peristalsis			
Stomach			
Small intestine			
Large intestine			

Action plan: **What I need to do to improve my learning** _____

_____

_____

_____

_____

TRANSPORT IN THE BODY

Log onto **www.edcolearning.ie** to find the **Mind Map** for this chapter.

Homework questions

1 The diagram represents a blood sample.

Which of the labelled parts carries out the following functions?

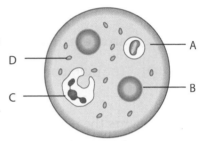

(a) Transports heat _____

(b) Attacks disease-causing organisms _____

(c) Transports food _____

(d) Forms blood clots _____

(e) Contains haemoglobin _____

2

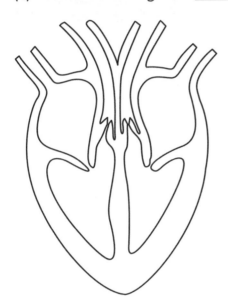

(a) On the diagram use blue arrows to show the path of low-oxygen blood.

(b) On the diagram use red arrows to show the path of high-oxygen blood.

3 (a) On the diagram use red arrows to show the path of oxygen-rich blood.

(b) On the diagram use blue arrows to show the path of oxygen-poor blood.

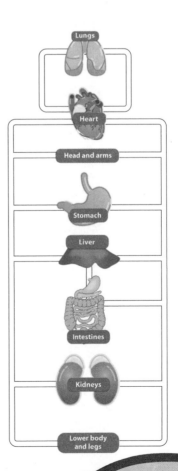

4 Use the correct words from the list below to complete the following sentences.

| bone marrow | lungs | capillaries | white blood cells | arteries | plasma | heart |

(a) The liquid part of blood is called _____.

(b) Red blood cells are made in _____.

(c) Antibodies are made by _____.

(d) _____ carry blood away from the heart.

(e) Arteries and veins are connected by _____.

(f) The pulmonary artery carries blood from the _____ to the _____.

5 Rewrite the words from the following list into the correct spaces in column B of the table below to match the descriptions in column A.

| left ventricle | haemoglobin | capillaries | right ventricle | valves | pulse |

Column A	Column B
Carries oxygen in red blood cells	
The smallest type of blood vessels	
Control the flow of blood	
The chamber of the heart that pumps blood around the body	
The chamber of the heart that pumps blood to the lungs	
The pressure of blood on the wall of an artery	

6 The diagram represents the circulatory system.

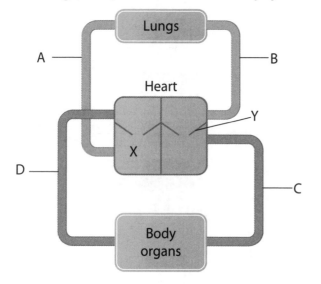

(a) Name the blood vessel labelled A.

_____

(b) Is blood vessel C an artery or a vein? Explain your answer.

_____

_____

(c) Name the heart chamber labelled X.

_____

(d) Name the structure labelled Y.

_____

(e) Which labelled blood vessel has the lowest concentration of oxygen?

_____

7 The diagram shows a section through a human heart.

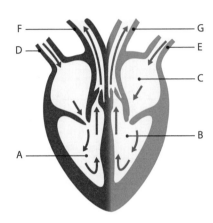

(a) Name the parts labelled A–G.

A _____

B _____

C _____

D _____

E _____

F _____

G _____

(b) Match one of the letters from the diagram with each of the following definitions:

(i) The chamber that pumps blood to the legs _____

(ii) The chamber that pumps blood to the lungs _____

(iii) The blood vessel that takes blood to the heart from the lungs _____

(iv) The blood vessel with the highest pressure _____

(v) The chamber that pumps blood to the left ventricle _____

(c) Compare the oxygen content of the blood in vessels E and D.

_____

_____

8 The table below shows the heart rates of two students taken very soon after four different activities.

		Activities			
		A	B	C	D
Heart rate (beats per minute)	Student X	110	75	105	65
	Student Y	130	85	95	70

(a) What was the pulse rate for:

(i) Student X after activity C? _____

(ii) Student Y after activity B? _____

(b) The four activities are listed below. Match these activities to the letters A, B, C and D in the table.

(i) Lying down _____

(ii) Sprinting _____

(iii) Jogging _____

(iv) Standing at rest _____

(c) Which activity showed the greatest difference in pulse rates between the two students?

_____

(d) How could the heart rates be measured?

_____

_____

(e) Why does exercise increase the heart rate?

_____

_____

_____

9 The diagram shows three types of blood vessels: A, B and C.

Wall   Thin wall

A   B   C

(a) Name each type of blood vessel:

A _____

B _____

C _____

(b) Why has vessel A got a very thick wall?

_____

(c) Vessel B often has valves to prevent blood flowing in the wrong direction, as shown in the diagram below.

Valve

X   Y

(i) In the diagram, is blood flowing from X to Y or from Y to X? _____

(ii) Is the heart closest to label X or Y?

_____

(iii) Why does blood vessel A not need valves?

_____

10 **Keywords.** Write one short sentence using each of the following words:

(a) Plasma _____

(b) Haemoglobin _____

(c) Antibodies _____

(d) Platelets _____

(e) Arteries _____

(f) Veins _____

(g) Capillaries _____

(h) Ventricles _____

(i) Atria _____

(j) Pulse _____

Activity 6.1: **What is our resting heart rate?**

(a) Date on which you carried out this activity _____

(b) In this activity what question did you ask yourself?

_____

(c) What predictions (hypothesis) did you make?

_____

_____

(d) How reliable and fair was your activity?

_____

(e) What safety features did you consider and what did you do to reduce the risks?

_____

_____

(f) Present your results in the following table:

Number of pulses per minute at rest	Total number of pulses in three minutes at rest	Average pulse rate per minute at rest

(g) Why did you record your pulse rate?

_____

_____

(h) Why did you record your pulse rate a number of times?

_____

_____

(i) What conclusion(s) did you reach?

_____

_____

_____

Activity 6.2: What is the effect of exercise on heart rate?

(a) Date on which you carried out this activity _____

(b) In this activity what question did you ask yourself?

_____

(c) What predictions (hypothesis) did you make?

_____

_____

_____

(d) How reliable and fair was your activity?

_____

_____

_____

(e) What safety features did you consider and what did you do to reduce the risks?

_____

_____

_____

(f) Present your results in the following table:

Number of pulses per minute at rest	Total number of pulses in 3 minutes at rest	Average pulse rate per minute at rest	Pulse rate per minute after exercise

(g) How long did it take for your pulse rate (which is the same as your heart rate) to return to its resting rate after the exercise was completed? _____

(h) What conclusion(s) did you reach?

_____

_____

_____

Reflection

(i) What are two things you liked about activities 6.1 and 6.2?

• _____

• _____

(j)   What did you find difficult about activities 6.1 and 6.2?

_____

_____

_____

(k)   If you were to do activities 6.1 and 6.2 again, what would you do differently?

_____

_____

_____

Self evaluation – Transport in the body

Now that you have completed this chapter, how well do you feel you understand each of the following (tick the relevant column)?

Topic	🙂	😐	🙁
Plasma			
Red blood cells			
White blood cells			
Platelets			
Heart			
Blood flow			
Pulse			
Finding the resting heart rate			
Investigating the effect of exercise on heart rate			
The path of blood around the body			

Action plan: What I need to do to improve my learning _____

_____

_____

_____

_____

_____

Log onto **www.edcolearning.ie** to find the **Mind Map** for this chapter.

Homework questions

1 Write the words from the box below into column B to match the function given in the first column. The first one has been completed for you.

| bronchiole | alveolus | inhaling | diaphragm | excretion | trachea | ~~diffusion~~ |

Function	Column B
The movement of molecules from a high to a low concentration	*Diffusion*
Breathing in	
A muscle that helps us to breathe	
Tiny air sac in the lungs	
The windpipe	
Getting rid of waste	
The tube directly connected to an alveolus	

2 Tick the relevant box for whether each of the following statements is true or false:

	True	False
(a) Oxygen is carried by white blood cells.	☐	☐
(b) We have more alveoli than lungs.	☐	☐
(c) There is more carbon dioxide in inhaled air than in exhaled air.	☐	☐
(d) Oxygen passes from the alveoli into the blood.	☐	☐
(e) The pulmonary artery carries blood to the heart.	☐	☐
(f) Limewater changes colour due to oxygen.	☐	☐
(g) Exhaled air is drier than inhaled air.	☐	☐

3 (a) Name the parts labelled A, B, C, D and E in the diagram.

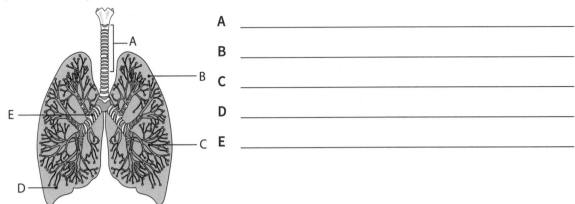

A _____

B _____

C _____

D _____

E _____

(b) Name one muscle used to get air into the lungs.

_____

4 Our lungs contain about 600 million tiny alveoli. The alveoli carry out gas exchange, as shown in the diagram.

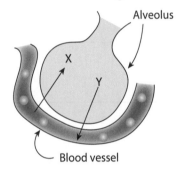

During gas exchange gas X leaves the blood vessel and enters the alveolus. At the same time gas Y leaves the alveolus and enters the blood vessel.

(a) Name the type of blood vessel found surrounding the alveolus.

_____

(b) Name the process by which gas exchange takes place.

_____

(c) Name the gas X.

_____

(d) Name the gas Y.

_____

(e) Gas X is produced in a chemical reaction in living things. What is this chemical reaction called?

_____

(f) Why do we have so many alveoli?

_____

_____

5 The diagram shows a model of the breathing system.

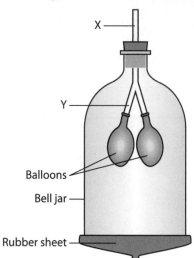

X

Y

Balloons

Bell jar

Rubber sheet

(a) Name the parts of the breathing system represented by:

(i) The balloons _____

(ii) The rubber sheet _____

(b) Tubes X and Y are hollow. What structures in the chest are represented by tube:

(i) X? _____

(ii) Y? _____

6 State a reason for each of the following:

(a) Exercise causes our breathing rate to increase.

_____

(b) There are tiny hairs in the nose.

_____

(c) The walls of the alveoli are very thin.

_____

(d) Our lungs are surrounded by huge numbers of blood capillaries.

_____

(e) We need two bronchi.

_____

7 The graph shows the breathing rate of a person before, during and after exercise. The exercise lasted 3 minutes, starting at minute one.

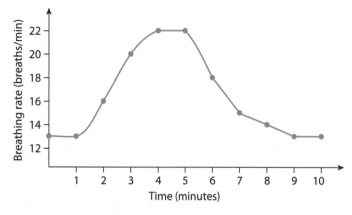

(a) What was the person's resting breathing rate? _____

(b) What was the person's maximum breathing rate? _____

(c) What was the person's breathing rate 2 minutes after the exercise started? _____

(d) Calculate the time taken for each breath at 3 minutes. _____

(e) How long did it take the person to return to their resting breathing rate after the exercise had stopped? _____

8 The table shows how a person's breathing rate changes at different concentrations of oxygen.

Oxygen concentration in the air (%)	13	14	15	16	17	18	19	20	21
Breathing rate (breaths per minute)	48	40	33	26	20	17	14	12	10

(a) Draw a graph of these values on the graph paper below with breathing rate on the y-axis and oxygen concentration in the air on the x-axis.

(b) State the relationship between oxygen concentration and breathing rate shown by these values. _____

_____

(c) Explain why the breathing rate changes as oxygen concentration changes.

_____

_____

(d) How does changing the oxygen concentration from 21% to 17% affect the breathing rate? _____

_____

9 Keywords. Write one short sentence using each of the following words:

(a) Respiration _____

(b) Excretion _____

(c) Trachea _____

(d) Bronchus _____

(e) Bronchiole _____

(f) Alveolus _____

(g) Diaphragm _____

(h) Inhaling _____

(i) Exhaling _____

Activity 7.1: What happens to our chests when we breathe?

(a) Date on which you carried out this activity _____

(b) In this activity what question did you ask yourself?

_____

(c) What did you feel as you breathed in?

_____

(d) How did your hand position change?

_____

(e) Did your chest get bigger or smaller as you breathed in?

_____

(f) How did your chest change when you exhaled?

_____

(g) What conclusion(s) did you reach?

_____

_____

_____

Activity 7.2: Can a model of the chest show how we get air in and out of the lungs?

(a) Date on which you carried out this activity _____

(b) In this activity what question did you ask yourself?

_____

(c) What happened to the size of the balloon when you pulled down on the plastic cover?

_____

(d) What happened to the size of the balloon when you pushed up on the plastic cover?

_____

(e) What conclusion(s) did you reach?

_____

_____

_____

In this investigation:

(f) The plastic cover represents the _____

(g) The balloon represents the _____

(h) Pushing up on the plastic cover represents _____

(i) Pulling down on the plastic cover represents _____

Activity 7.3: Can we compare the carbon dioxide levels of inhaled and exhaled air?

(a) Date on which you carried out this activity _____

(b) In this activity what question did you ask yourself?

_____

(c) Record your results. Tick one of the boxes below to show the result you got in this activity.

The limewater turned milky first in the test tube that I:

Breathed in through ☐

Breathed out through. ☐

(d) What conclusion(s) did you reach? What does this activity tell us about the composition of the air breathed in and out?

_____

_____

_____

Activity 7.4: How can we find our breathing rate at rest?

(a) Date on which you carried out this activity _____

(b) In this activity what question did you ask yourself?

_____

(c) Record your results in the following table.

Number of inhalations (breaths) per minute at rest	Total number of inhalations (breaths) in 3 minutes at rest	Average number of inhalations (breaths) per minute at rest

(d) What conclusion(s) did you reach?

_____

_____

_____

(e) Why did you record your breathing rate a number of times?

_____

_____

Activity 7.5: How can we investigate the effect of exercise on the rate of breathing?

(a) Date on which you carried out this activity _____

(b) In this activity what question did you ask yourself?

_____

(c) What prediction did you make?

_____

(d) Record your results in the following table:

Number of inhalations (breaths) per minute at rest	Total number of inhalations (breaths) in 3 minutes at rest	Average breathing rate per minute at rest	Breathing rates per minute after exercise

(e) What conclusion(s) did you reach?

_____

_____

_____

(f) How long did it take for your breathing rate to return to its resting rate after the exercise was completed?

_____

_____

_____

Reflection

(g) What are two things you liked about activities 7.1–7.5?

• _____

• _____

(h) **What did you find difficult about these activities?**

_____

_____

_____

(i) **If you were to do these activities again, what would you do differently?**

_____

_____

_____

Self evaluation – The breathing system

Now that you have completed this chapter, how well do you feel you understand each of the following (tick the relevant column)?

Topic	🙂	😐	🙁
What happens when we breathe			
The parts of the breathing system			
What happens in the alveoli			
The difference between air breathed in and air breathed out			
Investigating the carbon dioxide levels of air breathed in and air breathed out			
Why exercise affects breathing rates			
Measuring breathing rates			

Action plan: What I need to do to improve my learning _____

_____

_____

_____

_____

_____

CHAPTER 8

THE STUDY OF A HABITAT

Log onto **www.edcolearning.ie** to find the **Mind Map** for this chapter.

Homework questions

1   Answer the following questions in relation to your investigation of a habitat.

(a)   Name the type of ecosystem your habitat represented.

_____

(b)   You measured some abiotic factors. What is meant by the term 'abiotic factor'?

_____

(c)   Name two abiotic factors you measured.

_____

_____

(d)   Name the apparatus you used or describe how you measured one of the abiotic factors you listed in part (c) above.

_____

_____

_____

2   Both of the pieces of equipment shown in the diagram are used to collect animals in a habitat study.

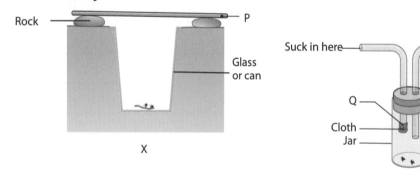

(a)   Select the correct name for each piece of equipment from the list below.

beating tray   quadrat   pooter   pitfall trap

X is called a _____

Y is called a _____

(b)   Explain how you used the two pieces of apparatus.

X _____

Y _____

(c) One of the pieces of apparatus in the list in part (a) is not used to collect animals. Name this piece of apparatus.

_____

(d) What is the function of the structures labelled P and Q in the diagram?

P _____

Q _____

(e) Why did you collect animals in the habitat?

_____

_____

3 To estimate the number of plants in a field, students used a square framed device. They placed it at random ten times in the field. On each occasion they listed the plants that were visible in the square frame. Their results are given below.

	1	2	3	4	5	6	7	8	9	10	Frequency
Ryegrass	✓	✗	✓	✓	✓	✗	✓	✓	✓	✓	
Primrose	✗	✓	✗	✗	✓	✓	✗	✗	✗	✗	
Nettle	✓	✗	✓	✗	✗	✓	✗	✗	✓	✗	

(a) Name the square framed device the students used.

_____

(b) How might the students have ensured that the device was placed at random?

_____

_____

(c) Why was the device placed in so many different locations?

_____

_____

_____

(d) Calculate the frequency for each of the three plants and place your answers in the frequency column in the table above.

4 The diagram shows a food web for a woodland habitat.

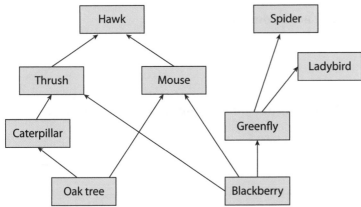

(a) Name the producers in this web.

_____

_____

(b) Is the greenfly a producer or a consumer? _____

(c) Is the caterpillar a herbivore, a carnivore or an omnivore? _____

(d) Write out a food chain from this web that involves four organisms.

_____

(e) If the number of mice decreased in this habitat, what do you think would happen to the number of hawks?

_____

(f) What do mice and thrushes compete for in this food web? _____

(g) How many food chains is the mouse involved in? _____

(h) How many different types of animals feed on the blackberry? _____

(i) How would you collect greenflies?

_____

_____

5 The diagram represents how materials recycle in a habitat.

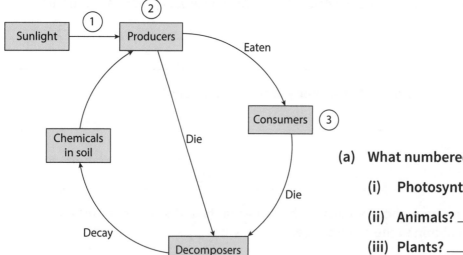

(a) What numbered point represents:

(i) Photosynthesis? _____

(ii) Animals? _____

(iii) Plants? _____

(b) Name two types of organisms that act as decomposers.

(i) _____

(ii) _____

(c) What problem would there be for plants in a habitat that did not contain any decomposers?

_____

_____

6 To study the number of robins in a hedgerow habitat, scientists trapped, counted and released robins at different times of the year. Their results are given in the following graph.

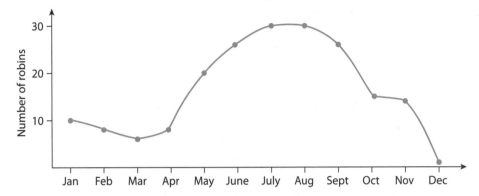

Looking at the graph, answer the following questions.

(a) What month(s) had the greatest number of robins? _____

(b) What month had the lowest number of robins? _____

(c) In what month were there 20 robins? _____

(d) Give a reason for the increase in the number of robins between March and July.

_____

(e) Suggest a reason for the decline in the number of robins between August and December.

_____

7 **Keywords.** Write one short sentence using each of the following words:

(a) Ecosystem _____

(b) Habitat _____

(c) Environmental (abiotic) factors _____

(d) Identification key _____

(e) Adaptations _____

(f) Community _____

(g) Competition _____

(h) Interdependence _____

(i) Food chain _____

(j) Food web _____

(k) Energy flow _____

(l) Matter flow _____

(a)   Date on which you carried out this activity _____

(b)   In this activity what question did you ask yourself?

_____

(c)   What prediction (hypothesis) did you make?

_____

_____

(d)   Name the plants shown in **Figure 8.4** of the textbook (page 80).

A is _____   B is _____

C is _____   D is _____

(e)   Name the animals shown in **Figure 8.5** of the textbook (page 80).

A is _____   B is _____

C is _____   D is _____

E is _____   F is _____

Activity 8.2: How can we collect plants and animals in a habitat?

(a)   Date on which you carried out this activity _____

(b)   Record your results in the following table:

Name of collection apparatus used	Organisms collected

(c)   Name five plants you found in your habitat study.

_____

_____

(d)   Name five animals you found in your habitat study.

_____

_____

(e) What observations did (or might) you find to suggest that animals that you could not see were present in the habitat?

_____

_____

Activity 8.3: **How can we estimate the number of plants in a habitat?**

(a) Date on which you carried out this activity _____

(b) Record your results in the table below:

Names of plants	Quadrat number										Total	% frequency
	1	2	3	4	5	6	7	8	9	10		

(c) Present the data you collected in the table in the form of a bar chart.

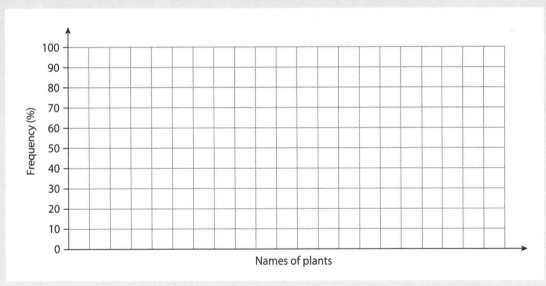

Answer the following questions using examples of organisms you found in your habitat study.

(d) (i) Name any plant adaptation. _____

(ii) State the benefit of the named adaptation. _____

_____

(e) (i) Name any animal adaptation. _____

(ii) State the benefit of the named adaptation. _____

_____

(f) (i) Give an example of competition in your habitat study. _____

_____

(ii) What were the organisms competing for? _____

(g) (i) Give an example of interdependence in your habitat study.

_____

(ii) Explain how each of the organisms you named at (i) above depended on the other.

_____

_____

(h) Name a producer you found in your habitat study. _____

(i) Name a consumer you found in your habitat study. _____

(j) Name a herbivore you found in your habitat study. _____

(k) Name a carnivore you found in your habitat study. _____

(l) Name an omnivore you found in your habitat study. _____

(m) Name a decomposer you found in your habitat study. _____

(n) Give an example of a food chain from the habitat you studied.

_____

(o) In the box below give an example of a food web from the habitat that you studied.

Self evaluation – The study of a habitat

Now that you have completed this chapter, how well do you feel you understand each of the following (tick the relevant column)?

Topic	🙂	😐	🙁
The difference between an ecosystem and a habitat			
Measuring environmental factors			
How to use a key			
How to collect organisms			
How to estimate the number of plants in a habitat			
Adaptations			
Competition			
Producers, consumers and decomposers			
Food chains			
Food web			
Energy flow			
Matter flow			

Action plan: What I need to do to improve my learning _____

_____

_____

_____

_____

CHAPTER 9
FACTORS AFFECTING HUMAN HEALTH

Log onto **www.edcolearning.ie** to find the **Mind Map** for this chapter.

Homework questions

1 Health is often described as a state of physical and mental well-being.

(a) What is meant by 'physical well-being'?

_____

_____

(b) What is meant by 'mental well-being'?

_____

_____

2 (a) Name the three main types of micro-organism.

_____

(b) State one negative feature of micro-organisms.

_____

(c) State one benefit of micro-organisms. _____

_____

(d) Antibiotics are used to treat tuberculosis but are of no value in treating measles.

(i) Is the statement above true or false? _____

(ii) Give a reason for your answer.

_____

3 Tick the relevant box for whether each of the following statements is true or false:

	True	False
(a) A person who does not have an infection may be unhealthy.	☐	☐
(b) Some people are less healthy due to the genes they inherit.	☐	☐
(c) Proteins are needed to form hair and nails.	☐	☐
(d) We should eat more meat and fish than fruit and vegetables.	☐	☐
(e) Smoking damages our heart and lungs.	☐	☐
(f) Exercise makes us tired in the short term but gives us more energy in the long term.	☐	☐
(g) Alcohol is never addictive.	☐	☐
(h) All micro-organisms are harmful.	☐	☐
(i) Antibiotics are made in the body.	☐	☐

4 Answer the following questions based on your completed food chart from question 9.31 in the textbook.

(a) Name any of the food groups that you eat too much of.

_____

_____

(b) Name any of the food groups that you eat too little of.

_____

_____

(c) What changes to your diet (if any) do you need to make?

_____

_____

5 Haemochromatosis is a disorder in which the body stores too much iron. It is caused by a single gene. The dominant version of the gene (H) means the person is normal. If a person has the genetic combination Hh they are normal but are described as carriers. A person with haemochromatosis has the genetic combination hh.

In a family both parents are normal. However, their first child has haemochromatosis.

(a) Fill in the spaces below to represent this family.

Parents ( ) x ( )

Possible gametes ( ) and ( ) x ( ) and ( )

Possible genetic
combinations of children ( ), ( ), ( ), ( )

Normal or
Haemochromatosis _____, _____, _____, _____

(b) What is the percentage chance that the next child of this couple will be normal?

_____

(c) Why is haemochromatosis considered to be a genetic disorder?

_____

(d) Is haemochromatosis an inherited condition? Explain your answer.

_____

_____

(e) Give one reason why humans need iron. _____

_____

6 You are a writer for your school magazine. You have been asked to write an article on one of the following topics.

(a) The impact of bodybuilding on teenage health

(b) Sun creams are a waste of money

(c) Ultraviolet (UV) radiation is bad for our health

(d) Fast food restaurants should be banned from locations close to schools

(e) Are super foods a super scam?

(f) Portion sizes are one of the greatest contributors leading to obesity in young people

(g) Smoking is one of the greatest causes of ill-health

(h) A health-related topic of your own choice

Name the title of your article and outline the arguments for or against it with reference to a media-based argument. (This article could easily form the basis of your Classroom-Based Assessment, CBA2).

Title: _____

_____

_____

_____

_____

_____

_____

_____

_____

_____

_____

_____

_____

_____

_____

_____

_____

_____

_____

7 The bar chart shows the number of deaths per year from lung cancer in five different countries.

Answer the following questions based on the chart.

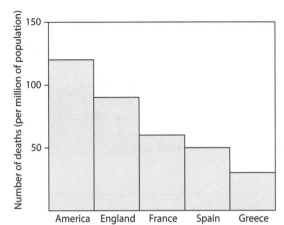

(a) If the population of Spain is 45 million, how many people are expected to die of lung cancer each year in Spain?

_____

(b) Which country would you expect to have the lowest number of cigarette smokers?

_____

(c) The population of Ireland is 5 million and England's population is 50 million. How many people are expected to die each year in Ireland from lung cancer if our death rate is the same as England's? Show your calculations in reaching your answer.

_____

_____

8 The graph shows the number of deaths (per 100 000 of population) from tuberculosis and from heart disease in Ireland from 1949 to 1999.

(a) What was the number of deaths per 100 000 from tuberculosis in:

   (i) 1949? _____

   (ii) 1999? _____

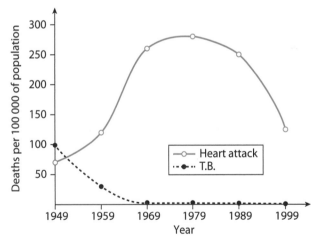

(b) Suggest a reason for the change in numbers in part (a) above.

_____

_____

(c) What was the first year more people died of heart disease than of tuberculosis?

_____

(d) The rate of death by heart disease increased from 1949 to 1979. Suggest reasons for such a rise in deaths.

_____

_____

(e) Why, do you think, did the rate of death from heart disease decline from 1979 to 1999?

_____

_____

9 **Keywords.** Write one short sentence using each of the following words:

(a) Health _____

(b) Single-gene disorders _____

(c) Multi-gene disorders _____

(d) Balanced diet/food pyramid _____

(e) Food energy values _____

(f) Micro-organisms _____

(g) Viruses _____

(h) Parasites _____

(i) Pathogens _____

(j) Antibodies _____

(k) Bacteria _____

(l) Antibiotics _____

(m) Vaccination _____

(n) Immunisation _____

Activity 9.1: **How can we show that micro-organisms are present in different locations?**

(a)   **Date on which you carried out this activity** _____

(b)   **In this activity what question did you ask yourself?** _____

_____

(c)   **What prediction (hypothesis) did you make?** _____

_____

(d)   **How reliable and fair was your activity?** _____

_____

(e)   **What safety features did you consider and what did you do to reduce the risks?**

_____

_____

(f)   **Record your results in the following table.**

Observation	Location
Greatest number of different types of micro-organisms	
Least number of different types of micro-organisms	
The dish(es) with the most overall growth	
Dish(es) with no visible growth	
Control dish	

(g)   **What conclusion(s) did you reach?**

_____

_____

_____

Reflection

(h)   **What are two things you liked about this activity?**

•   _____

•   _____

(i)   **What did you find difficult about this activity?**

_____

(j)   **If you were to do this activity again, what would you do differently?**

_____

_____

(k) In this **chapter** what did you learn that was new about how health is affected by:

  (i) Inherited factors? _____

  _____

  (ii) Environmental factors? _____

  _____

  (iii) Nutrition? _____

  _____

  (iv) Lifestyle choices? _____

  _____

(l) What did you learn about the role of micro-organisms in human health?

  _____

Evaluation

(m) Answer the following questions with respect to your answers to either question 9.16 or 9.28 in the textbook. State which question you are answering.

  I am referring to question _____

  (i) Compared to other groups in the class, was your group's work: better / about the same / not as good? _____

  (ii) What could your group do to improve your work? _____

  _____

  (iii) If you were doing this group work again, what might you do differently?

  _____

  _____

(n) If you presented your group's work to the class, answer the following questions:

  (i) Did you enjoy the experience? Give reasons for your answer.

  _____

  _____

  (ii) If you were to present the information to another class, what would you do differently?

  _____

  _____

Self evaluation – Factors affecting human health

Now that you have completed this chapter, how well do you feel you understand each of the following (tick the relevant column)?

Topic	🙂	😐	🙁
Inherited factors affecting health			
The effects of nutrition on health			
How smoking affects health			
How exercise affects health			
The effects of alcohol and drugs on health			
The value of sleep and a proper work/life balance for health			
The effect of viruses, bacteria and fungi on health			
How to show micro-organisms are present in different locations			

Action plan: **What I need to do to improve my learning** _____

_____

_____

_____

_____

_____

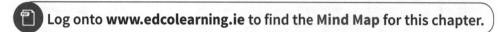

Log onto **www.edcolearning.ie** to find the **Mind Map** for this chapter.

Homework questions

1 Use the words in the box to complete the following sentences.

alcohol	anaerobic	lactic acid	energy	water

Respiration is the release of _____ from food. Aerobic respiration needs oxygen while _____ respiration does not use oxygen.

In aerobic respiration the end products are carbon dioxide and _____.

In anaerobic respiration in humans _____ is produced.

In anaerobic respiration in yeast the end products are _____ and carbon dioxide.

2 The diagram represents aerobic respiration. Answer the questions below, based on the diagram.

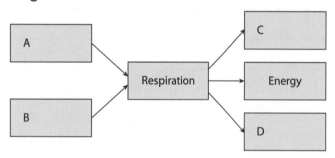

(a) What substances are represented by the letters A, B, C and D?

A _____ B _____

C _____ D _____

(b) Where in the human body does respiration take place?

_____

(c) What is the benefit of respiration to living things?

_____

_____

3 Give word equations for:

(a) Aerobic respiration

_____

(b) Anaerobic respiration in muscle

_____

(c) Anaerobic respiration in yeast

_____

4 Use the words in the box to complete the following sentences.

| food | sunlight | aerobic | chlorophyll | glucose |

In photosynthesis energy from _____ is used to combine carbon

dioxide and water together to form a sugar called _____

and the gas oxygen. This reaction only takes place if the green pigment called

_____ is present.

The main benefits of photosynthesis are that it makes _____ for the

plant and it forms oxygen which is needed by living things for _____

respiration.

5 (a) List three factors that affect respiration.

_____

(b) Explain why respiration slows down above a certain temperature.

_____

_____

6 A compost heap contains grass cuttings and leaves. A scientist measured the temperature of
the air and in the compost heap at the same time each day for 7 weeks.

The table shows the average temperature of the air and in the compost heap each week
over the 7 weeks.

Week number	1	2	3	4	5	6	7
Air temperature (°C)	10	12	14	11	13	12	14
Compost temperature (°C)	10	13	20	34	44	42	30

(a) How did the scientist measure the temperatures over the course of the investigation?

_____

(b) How did the scientist calculate the average weekly temperature?

_____

(c) Why did the air temperature vary over the 7 weeks?

_____

(d) Give one precaution the scientist might take when measuring the temperature of the compost heap.

_____

_____

(e) Why did the temperature in the compost heap rise from week 1 to week 5?

_____

(f) Suggest why the temperature in the compost heap fell in the final 2 weeks.

_____

7 (a) List three factors that affect photosynthesis.

_____

(b) Insert the letter T or F after each of the following statements to say if it is true or false.

Statement	True or false
Respiration takes place in the light	
Respiration takes place in the dark	
Photosynthesis takes place in the light	
Photosynthesis takes place in the dark	
Respiration makes food	
Photosynthesis makes food	

8 Give two reasons why life on Earth would be impossible without photosynthesis.

(a) _____

(b) _____

9 To investigate the effect of temperature on the rate of photosynthesis the equipment was set up as shown in the diagram.

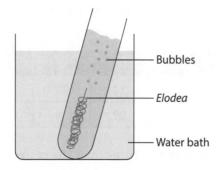

Elodea (pondweed) is an underwater plant. The number of bubbles/minute was counted at each temperature and the results are given in the table.

Temperature (°C)	5	10	15	20	25	30	35
Number of bubbles/minute	3	8	15	25	30	30	20

(a) What is the main gas in the bubbles? _____

(b) Use the graph paper below to draw a graph of the results.

(c) Why should the light source be kept at the same distance from the equipment throughout the experiment?

_____

_____

(d) How is the rate of photosynthesis measured in this activity?

_____

_____

(e) Based on these results, at what temperature is photosynthesis at its maximum rate?

_____

10 Keywords. Write one short sentence using each of the following words:

(a) Respiration _____

(b) Aerobic respiration _____

(c) Enzyme _____

(d) Anaerobic respiration _____

(e) Lactic acid _____

(f) Photosynthesis _____

(g) Solar energy _____

(h) Chemical energy _____

(i) Stomata _____

(j) Chlorophyll _____

Activity 10.1: **Can we investigate a factor that affects respiration?**

(a) Date on which you carried out this activity _____

(b) In this activity what factor did you change? _____

_____

(c) What predictions (hypothesis) did you make? _____

_____

(d) How reliable and fair was your activity? _____

_____

(e) What safety features did you consider and what did you do to reduce the risks?

_____

_____

(f) Identify controls in the activity. _____

_____

(g) Identify any relevant variables in the activity. _____

_____

(h) Record your results in the following table.

Temperature (°C)	10	20	30	40
Volume of foam produced (ml)				

(i) What conclusion(s) did you reach? _____

_____

(j) What result would you expect in the control activity?

_____

_____

Activity 10.2: **Can we show that a gas is produced by respiration in yeast?**

(a) Date on which you carried out this activity _____

(b) In this activity what question did you ask yourself?

_____

(c) What predictions (hypothesis) did you make?

_____

_____

(d) Record your results in the following table.

Contents of bottle	Amount of expansion of balloon (e.g. none / some / most)
Water, yeast, sugar	
Water, yeast (no sugar)	

(e) What conclusion(s) did you reach?

_____

_____

Reflection

(f) What are two things you liked about this activity?

• _____

• _____

(g) What did you find difficult about this activity?

_____

_____

(h) If you were to do this activity again, what would you do differently?

_____

_____

Activity 10.3: **Can we investigate a factor that affects photosynthesis?**

(a) Date on which you carried out this activity _____

(b) Record your results in the following table.

	Leaf in the light	Leaf in the dark
Final colour of the leaf		

(c) What factor did you change in this investigation?

_____

(d) How did you change the factor you named above?

_____

(e) How did you know whether photosynthesis was affected?

_____

_____

(f) What conclusion did you reach?

_____

_____

Self evaluation – Respiration and photosynthesis

Now that you have completed this chapter, how well do you feel you understand each of the following (tick the relevant column)?

Topic	😊	😐	☹
Aerobic respiration			
Anaerobic respiration			
Factors that affect respiration			
The products of respiration			
How to show that respiration produces energy			
How to show that a gas is produced by respiration in yeast			
Photosynthesis			
Factors that affect photosynthesis			
The products of photosynthesis			

Action plan: What I need to do to improve my learning _____

_____

_____

_____

_____

_____

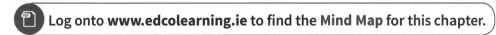

HUMAN REPRODUCTION

Log onto **www.edcolearning.ie** to find the **Mind Map** for this chapter.

Homework questions

1   The diagram shows the reproductive system of a human male.

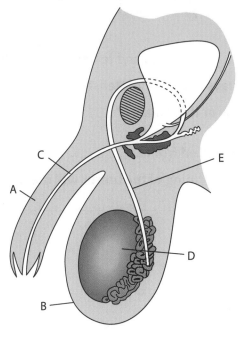

(a) Name the parts labelled A, B, C, D and E.

A _____

B _____

C _____

D _____

E _____

(b) Name the labelled part in which sperm are produced. _____

(c) Give one difference between a sperm and an egg.

_____

_____

(d) What is the role of the tail in a sperm?

_____

_____

2   The diagram shows the reproductive system of a human female.

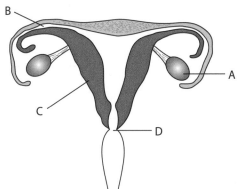

(a) Name the parts labelled A, B, C and D.

A _____

B _____

C _____

D _____

(b) Name the labelled part in which:

(i)   Eggs are formed _____

(ii) Fertilisation takes place _____

(iii) Implantation takes place _____.

(c) Name the cell produced as a result of fertilisation. _____

3   Insert the words from the box into the correct spaces in the following passage.

menstruation	maturity	14	pregnant	28	ovary	1

Puberty is the age of sexual _____ in males and females. Normally

a menstrual cycle will take place once every _____ days in a female. Menstrual cycles

do not take place before puberty, after the menopause or if a female is _____.

During each menstrual cycle an egg develops and is released from an _____

on day _____. On day 28 if the female is not pregnant the lining of the uterus will break

down and pass out of the female. This is called _____.

The first day of menstruation marks day _____ of a new cycle.

4   (a) What are gametes?

   _____

(b) Name the male gametes.

   _____

(c) Where are the male gametes formed?

   _____

(d) Name the female gametes.

   _____

(e) Where are the female gametes formed?

   _____

5   Name the parts of the female reproductive system in which the following take place.

(a) Eggs are formed

   _____

(b) Sperm enter the female system

   _____

(c) Eggs and sperm normally meet

   _____

(d) The baby normally develops during pregnancy

   _____

6 (a) The fusion of a sperm and an egg is called _____.

(b) The cell formed due to fertilisation is called the _____.

(c) The attaching of the ball of cells onto the lining of the womb is called _____.

(d) The membrane surrounding the developing foetus is called the _____.

(e) The liquid surrounding the developing baby is called _____ fluid.

7 The diagram shows a foetus in the uterus.

Amniotic fluid

B

A

C

(a) Name the parts labelled A, B and C on the diagram.

A _____

B _____

C _____

(b) What is the benefit of amniotic fluid?

_____

_____

(c) What evidence is there to suggest that the baby is about to be born?

_____

_____

(d) Why do pregnant women have to be very careful in taking medications?

_____

_____

8 You have been asked to design an information leaflet on the benefits of breastfeeding. List some of the main points that should be included in the leaflet.

• _____

• _____

• _____

• _____

• _____

• _____

9 Answer the following questions about contraception.

(a) What is contraception? _____

_____

(b) Give one reason in favour of contraception. _____

_____

(c) Give one reason against contraception. _____

_____

10 Answer the following questions about IVF.

(a) What is IVF? _____

_____

(b) Give one reason in favour of IVF. _____

_____

(c) Give one reason against IVF. _____

_____

11 Answer the following questions about stem cells.

(a) What are stem cells? _____

_____

(b) Give one reason in favour of using stem cells. _____

_____

(c) Give one reason against using stem cells. _____

_____

12 (a) Name the cord that attaches the baby's navel to the placenta. _____

(b) The placenta is found between the umbilical cord and the lining of the _____.

(c) Why can a baby in the womb not breathe using their lungs?

_____

(d) How does a baby in the womb get oxygen?

_____

(e) Name a waste substance that passes across the placenta from the baby to the mother.

_____

(f) Very often the baby of a drug-addicted mother is born with a similar addiction.

Why does this happen? _____

_____

13 Read the following extract and answer the questions that follow.

In 1979 China realised that its population was growing far too fast. They established a 'one child policy', which meant that each couple could only have one child. By agreeing to this policy the family gained more access to education, more healthcare and more childcare.

There were substantial problems in enacting the policy. If a couple had more than one child they were fined. In rural areas people were used to having large families and did not want to be limited to having only one child. It was difficult to enforce the policy in rural areas and was easier to enforce in cities. Many women were forced to have abortions and to be sterilised if they became pregnant after having one child.

This policy resulted in a fall in the birth rate and a resulting decrease in the growth of the population. However, some problems arose. Due to a long-established liking for boys large numbers of female children were sent to orphanages, became homeless or were killed. Up to 90% of abortions were female foetuses. All of this has resulted in the gender balance in China swinging in favour of men. There are now about 60 million more men than women in China.

In recent years China has adapted their one child policy. If the first born child is female the couple can apply for permission to have a second child. This also applies if both parents are single children.

The population of China is now increasing much more slowly. It still has a huge population (1.3 billion in 2017, 17% of the world's population). China is now afraid that its population will fall. This will mean that there will be a smaller number of young, working people to support an older population.

(a) What is meant by 'China's one-child policy'? _____
_____
_____

(b) Why did China introduce the one-child policy? _____
_____

(c) State one advantage of this policy. _____
_____

(d) State one disadvantage of this policy. _____
_____

(e) Why does China now have fewer females than males? _____
_____

(f) Do you think orphanages in China have an equal balance of male and female children? Support your answer with evidence from this article.
_____
_____
_____

(g) Would you like to see a similar one-child policy introduced in Ireland? Explain your answer. _____

_____

_____

14 Keywords. Write one short sentence using each of the following words:

(a) Gametes _____

(b) Puberty _____

(c) Menstrual cycle/menstruation _____

(d) Ovulation _____

(e) Fertilisation _____

(f) Implantation _____

(g) Amniotic fluid _____

(h) Placenta _____

(i) Umbilical cord _____

(j) Stem cells _____

Self evaluation – Human reproduction

Now that you have completed this chapter, how well do you feel you understand each of the following (tick the relevant column)?

Topic	🙂	😐	🙁
The male reproductive system			
The female reproductive system			
The menstrual cycle			
Fertilisation			
Pregnancy			
The placenta			
Birth			
Contraception			
In vitro fertilisation			
Stem cells			

Action plan: What I need to do to improve my learning _____

_____

CHAPTER 12

MAINTAINING BIODIVERSITY, BENEFITS OF ECOSYSTEMS AND GLOBAL FOOD PRODUCTION

 Log onto **www.edcolearning.ie** to find the **Mind Map** for this chapter.

Homework questions

1. (a) What is meant by the term 'conservation'?

_____

_____

(b) Give four benefits of good conservation practices.

(i) _____

(ii) _____

(iii) _____

(iv) _____

2. (a) What is meant by the term 'biodiversity'?

_____

_____

(b) Give four causes of the loss of biodiversity.

_____

_____

_____

_____

3. (a) What is pollution?

_____

_____

(b) Give an example of how you, or your family, may contribute to each of the following:

(i) Air pollution

_____

_____

(ii) Water pollution

_____

_____

(iii) Soil or land pollution

_____

_____

4 The Green Revolution produced more food. Tick the relevant box for whether each of the following features of the Green Revolution is a benefit or a disadvantage.

	Benefit	Disadvantage
(a) Food prices fell.	❏	❏
(b) Increased use of farm machinery caused increased unemployment.	❏	❏
(c) More water was used to grow crops.	❏	❏
(d) Crop yields were more reliable.	❏	❏
(e) Crops had shorter growing seasons.	❏	❏
(f) New crops were more easily damaged by diseases.	❏	❏
(g) Different crops resulted in more varied diets.	❏	❏
(h) Increased use of fertilisers caused more pollution.	❏	❏

5 **(a)** In what ways does human activity lead to the extinction of a species?

_____

_____

(b) What disadvantage might arise for humans if a plant species became extinct?

_____

_____

(c) How can we protect species from extinction?

_____

_____

6 What do the initials CITES, WWF and IWC stand for in relation to international conservation?

CITES = _____

WWF = _____

IWC = _____

7 At present hedges should be cut in Ireland only between September and February. This is to protect the habitat of nesting birds from destruction. However, with recent changes in climate the nesting season for birds is starting earlier each year. This is resulting in nests being destroyed by hedge-cutting, especially in February.

(a) How does hedge-cutting affect bird numbers?

_____

_____

(b) Why are birds nesting earlier now than in previous years?

_____

_____

(c) If nesting birds are to be fully protected, the ban on hedge-cutting should be changed to include a much longer period of the year (e.g. January to the end of October). What other problems might arise if hedges can be cut only for a much shorter period of time?

_____

_____

8 Give two examples of a substance in each case that can be:

(a) Reduced _____

(b) Reused _____

(c) Recycled _____

9 'National Parks support a rich biodiversity.'

(a) Explain why this statement is true.

_____

_____

(b) Outline the benefits of maintaining a rich biodiversity.

_____

_____

10 In terms of pollution and its effects on wildlife, write the events in the order in which they occur in the second column.

Random order of events	Correct order of events
(a) Earthworms eat fallen leaves from tree	
(b) Trees are sprayed with a chemical to kill insects	
(c) Small birds eat earthworms	
(d) Chemical spray is absorbed by tree leaves	
(e) Hawks eat small birds	
(f) Beetles kill trees by spreading a disease	
(g) Hawks are poisoned by chemical spray	

11 Read the following extract and answer the questions on the following page.

Global loss of plants and animals affecting Ireland

The global assessment of nature confirms that accelerating loss of plants and animals is affecting every part of the planet – Ireland included.

Human actions have already driven at least 680 vertebrate species to extinction since 1500, with many more likely to follow in coming decades according to an international study on extinction.

Intervention can work. Successful conservation efforts have saved from extinction at least 26 bird species and 6 ungulate species (large mammals, horses and rhinoceroses) including the Arabian Oryx and the Przewalski's horse. But the ability to save many species will not be possible based on current destruction of natural systems, the study warns.

▲ Figure 12.1 *The corncrake, known for its rasping call, was once widespread across the countryside, but the population was decimated by mechanised farming*

While the global assessment does not provide a country-by-country breakdown, the following Irish species are classified by scientists as under immediate threat; some are "critically endangered":

- European eel (due to pollution, dams on rivers, river drainage, poaching and climate change);

- Angel shark (probably less than 10 individuals are left, threatened by catch in nets set for crustaceans, notably the crawfish, which also happens to be endangered);

- Porbeagle shark, white skate, flapper skate, blue skate – all greatly diminished by bottom trawling, threatened now by fishing by catch and sea angling;

- Twenty-three types of moss and liverwort, eight types of water beetle, seven types of moth are critically endangered (CR);

- Five species of freshwater molluscs are CR due to land drainage, and pollution including the two species of freshwater pearl mussel, which are not reproducing in many of their rivers;

- Six types of bee are CR, mostly due to the lack of flowers in the countryside and pesticide use;

- Twenty species of plant are CR including the cloudberry (found from a single bog in County Tyrone), Irish fleabane (reduced to a single clump on the shores of Lough Derg) and the limestone fern (a single site in Mayo);

- No mammals are critically endangered but six species are already extinct including the grey wolf and the Irish elk.

Birds are not assessed in this way but BirdWatch Ireland highlights 37 species on their "red list" and of these the curlew, the ring ouzel, quail, nightjar, golden eagle, lapwing, golden plover, dunlin, redshank, corncrake and twite could be considered in imminent risk of extinction.

Source: courtesy of The Irish Wildlife Trust

(a) What is meant by the term 'vertebrate'? _____

_____

(b) How many vertebrate species have become extinct since 1500?

_____

(c) Name an Irish vertebrate that has become extinct since 1500.

_____

(d) What are the main threats to bees in Ireland? _____

_____

(e) Suggest why freshwater pearl mussels are not breeding as successfully as they once did. _____

_____

12 Keywords. Write one short sentence using each of the following words:

(a) Conservation _____

(b) Biodiversity _____

(c) Pollution _____

(d) Waste management _____

(e) Global food production _____

(f) Reduce _____

(g) Reuse _____

(h) Recycle _____

(i) Ecosystem _____

(j) Food gap _____

Activity 12.1: Can we purify water?

(a) Date on which you carried out this activity _____

(b) In this activity what question did you ask yourself? _____

(c) What prediction (hypothesis) did you make? _____

(d) How reliable and fair was your activity? _____

(e) What safety features did you consider and what did you do to reduce the risks?

_____

_____

(f)   Record your results: describe the appearance of the water (in terms of cloudy or clear) at the start and at the end of this activity in the following table.

	Original appearance	Final appearance
Unfiltered water (control)		
Filtered water		

(g)   What conclusion(s) did you reach?

_____

Reflection

(h)   What are two things you liked about this activity?

•   _____

•   _____

(i)   What did you find difficult about this activity?

_____

(j)   If you were to do this activity again, what would you do differently?

_____

Self evaluation – Maintaining biodiversity, benefits of ecosystems and global food production

Now that you have completed this chapter, how well do you feel you understand each of the following (tick the relevant column)?

Topic	🙂	😐	🙁
Conservation			
The need for conservation			
Habitat loss or fragmentation			
Pollution			
Waste management, the three Rs			
The benefits of ecosystems			
How water is purified			
Increasing global food production			
Increasing the amount of farmland			
Increasing crop yields			
Reducing the food gap			

Action plan: What I need to do to improve my learning _____

Peer Assessment

Date:__/__/__

_____   _____   _____
Your name   Name of lab partner   Title of work

Success Criteria	**How** did this piece of work achieve the success criteria?

Two excellent points	This could be improved by…
1	
2	

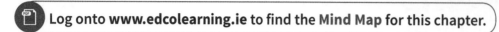

Log onto **www.edcolearning.ie** to find the **Mind Map** for this chapter.

Homework questions

1 **(a)** What is matter?

_____

_____

(b) Name the three states of matter.

(i) _____

(ii) _____

(iii) _____

2 Complete the following sentences:

(a) Solids have a definite _____.

(b) Liquids can _____ and hence do not have a definite _____.

(c) The particles in a solid are _____ and cannot easily move past each other.

(d) Liquids and solids have a definite _____ but gases do not.

3 What do we call these changes?

e.g. Liquid → **Gas** = **Boiling**

(a) Gas → Liquid = _____

(b) Solid → Liquid = _____

(c) Liquid → Solid = _____

4 Water boils at _____ °C and has a freezing point of _____ °C.

5 Write the correct term from the list in column 1 into the five spaces in columns 2 and 3 to complete the table:

Terms	State of matter	Property
Gases Cannot be compressed Solids No fixed shape No fixed volume	(i) _____	Definite shape Definite volume (iii) _____
	(ii) _____	Easily compressed (iv) _____ (v) _____

6 **Keywords.** Write one short sentence using each of the following words:

(a) Matter _____

(b) Atoms _____

(c) Volume _____

(d) Melting _____

(e) Boiling _____

(f) Evaporation _____

(g) Condensation _____

(h) Freezing _____

(i) Diffusion _____

Activity 13.1: How does matter change state?

(a) Date on which you carried out this activity _____

(b) In this activity what question did you ask yourself?

_____

(c) What predictions (hypothesis) did you make?

_____

_____

(d) How reliable and fair was your activity?

_____

_____

(e) What safety features did you consider and what did you do to reduce the risks?

_____

_____

(f) Identify controls in the activity.

_____

_____

(g) Identify any relevant dependent/independent/fixed variables in the activity.

_____

_____

(h) Draw a diagram of your apparatus.

(i) Record your results.

_____

_____

(j) **Melting**

    (i) What is happening to the particles in the solid when they are heated?

    _____

    _____

    Boiling

    (ii) What is happening to the particles when they change from a liquid to a gas?

    _____

    _____

    (iii) Do they require more energy than particles in a solid?

    _____

    _____

    Condensation

    (iv) What effect does the removal of energy have on the particles in the gas and why did it change into a liquid?

    _____

    _____

    (v) What is happening to the particles that has caused them to stop moving and form a solid?

    _____

    _____

Reflection

(k) What did you learn about each of the following? Fill in the table.

Melting	Boiling	Condensation	Freezing

(l) What conclusion(s) did you reach?

_____

_____

(m) What are two things you liked about this activity?

• _____

• _____

(n) What did you find difficult about this activity?

_____

_____

(o) If you were to do this activity again, what would you do differently?

_____

_____

Self evaluation – The particle theory

Now that you have completed this chapter, how well do you feel you understand each of the following (tick the relevant column)?

Topic	🙂	😐	🙁
Matter			
The three states of matter			
The particles in a solid			
The particles in a liquid			
The particles in a gas			
Changing substances from one state to another by heating or cooling them			
How particles are changed by melting			
How particles are changed by boiling			
How particles are changed by condensation			
How particles are changed by freezing			
Diffusion			

Action plan: What I need to do to improve my learning _____

_____

 Log onto **www.edcolearning.ie** to find the **Mind Map** for this chapter.

Homework questions

1 Complete the following:

A _____ change is one in which no new substance is formed. It is usually _____ to reverse, whereas in a _____ change a new substance is produced and it is usually _____ to reverse. Boiling water is an example of a _____ change.

2 Describe an activity you have done that involved:

(a) A chemical change

(b) A physical change.

For each one, explain how you decided whether the change involved was chemical or physical.

_____

_____

_____

_____

_____

3 What type of change(s) takes place when a candle is burning?

_____

4 Tick the correct box for whether each of the following changes is physical or chemical:

(a) A candle burning   Physical ☐   Chemical ☐

(b) A candle melting   Physical ☐   Chemical ☐

(c) A nail rusting   Physical ☐   Chemical ☐

(d) Switching on a torch   Physical ☐   Chemical ☐

(e) Squeezing oranges   Physical ☐   Chemical ☐

(f) An orange rotting   Physical ☐   Chemical ☐

(g) Milk going sour   Physical ☐   Chemical ☐

(h) Inflating a balloon   Physical ☐   Chemical ☐

(i) Freezing food   Physical ☐   Chemical ☐

5 **Keywords.** Write one short sentence using each of the following words:

(a) Chemical change _____

(b) Physical change _____

(c) Hydrochloric acid _____

(d) Sodium hydroxide _____

(e) Spatula _____

(f) Conservation _____

Activity 14.1: What changes are taking place in chemical reactions?

(a) Date on which you carried out this activity _____

(b) In this activity what question did you ask yourself?

_____

(c) What predictions (hypothesis) did you make?

_____

_____

(d) How reliable and fair was your activity?

_____

_____

(e) What safety features did you consider and what did you do to reduce the risks?

_____

_____

(f) Identify controls in the activity.

_____

_____

(g) Identify any relevant dependent/independent/fixed variables in the activity.

_____

_____

(h) Draw a diagram of your apparatus.

(i) Record your results.

_____

_____

(j) In which test tubes did a physical change take place and in which did a chemical change take place?

_____

_____

(k) Write down the properties that tell you if there has been a chemical reaction (chemical change).

_____

_____

(l) What conclusion(s) did you reach? _____

_____

Reflection

(m) What did you learn about each of the following?

Physical change	Chemical change

(n) What are two things you liked about this activity?

• _____

• _____

(o) What did you find difficult about this activity? _____

_____

Activity 14.2: Does mass change during physical changes and chemical changes?

(a) Date on which you carried out this activity _____

(b) In this activity what question did you ask yourself?

_____

(c) What predictions (hypothesis) did you make? _____

_____

(d) How reliable and fair was your activity? _____

_____

(e) What safety features did you consider and what did you do to reduce the risks?

_____

_____

(f) Identify controls in the activity.

_____

_____

(g) Identify any relevant dependent/independent/fixed variables in the activity.

_____

_____

(h) Draw a diagram of your apparatus.

(i) Record your results. _____

_____

(j) Did you notice any changes during reaction A and reaction B?

_____

_____

_____

_____

(k) What conclusion(s) did you reach? _____

Reflection

(l) What did you learn about mass during physical and chemical changes?

_____

_____

(m) What are two things you liked about this activity?

• _____

• _____

(n) What did you find difficult about this activity?

_____

_____

(o) If you were to do this activity again, what would you do differently?

_____

_____

Self evaluation – Observing change

Now that you have completed this chapter, how well do you feel you understand each of the following (tick the relevant column)?

Topic	☺	😐	☹
Physical change			
Chemical change			
Chemical reactions and their products			
The law of conservation of mass			

Action plan: What I need to do to improve my learning _____

_____

_____

CHAPTER 15

PARTICLES IN SOLUTION

📄 Log onto **www.edcolearning.ie** to find the **Mind Map** for this chapter.

Homework questions

1 Give two everyday examples of mixtures.

(i) _____

(ii) _____

2 Name two mixtures that can be separated by filtration.

(i) _____

(ii) _____

3 Name the parts labelled A, B, C, D and E on the diagram of the apparatus used to separate soil and water.

A _____

B _____

C _____

D _____

E _____

4 (a) Why is it not possible to separate a solution of salt and water by filtration?

_____

(b) Briefly describe how a sample of salt could be obtained from salty water.

_____

_____

_____

5 Match up, using arrows, the correct method to separate the mixture on the right of the following table.

Method	Mixture
Filtration	Salt and water
Distillation	Colours in a food dye
Chromatography	Chalk and water
Evaporation	Alcohol and water

6 Distillation is a technique used to separate _____ that have _____ boiling points.

7 During filtration the substance that is trapped in the filter paper is called the _____ and the liquid that passes through it is known as the _____ .

8 Select the correct term from the box on the right to complete the sentences below.

| Distillation |
| Condenser |
| Chromatography |
| Separated |
| Chromatography paper |
| Soluble |
| Insoluble |

To separate an ink into its various dyes we use a method called _____ .

Some dyes are carried further up the _____ than others. As a result, the dyes are _____ .

The dyes that are most _____ in the solvent are carried furthest up the chromatography paper.

9 **Keywords.** Write one short sentence using each of the following words:

(a) Solute _____

(b) Solvent _____

(c) Solution _____

(d) Soluble _____

(e) Insoluble _____

(f) Filtration _____

(g) Chromatography _____

(h) Distillation _____

Activity 15.1: How does temperature affect the solubility of a solute?

(a) Date on which you carried out this activity _____

(b) In this activity what question did you ask yourself?

_____

(c) What predictions (hypothesis) did you make? _____

_____

(d) How reliable and fair was your activity? _____

_____

(e) What safety features did you consider and what did you do to reduce the risks?

_____

_____

(f) Identify controls in the activity. _____

_____

(g) Identify any relevant dependent/independent/fixed variables in the activity.

_____

_____

(h) Draw a diagram of your apparatus.

(i) Record your results in the table below.

Temperature/°C	Mass (g) of sugar/100 cm³ of water	Mass (g) of salt/100 cm³ of water
Room temperature		
40		
60		
80		
100		

(j) 15.7 (a) How did the temperature affect the solubility of sugar and salt?

_____

_____

(k) 15.7 (b) What is the solubility of sugar at 55°C?

_____

(l) 15.7 (c) At what temperature will 30 g of salt dissolve in 100 cm³ of water?

_____

Reflection

(m) What are two things you liked about this activity?

- _____
- _____

(n) What did you find difficult about this activity?

_____

_____

(o) If you were to do this activity again, what would you do differently?

_____

_____

Separation of mixtures

Activity 15.2: Filtration

(a) Date on which you carried out this activity. _____

(b) What question did you ask yourself?

_____

(c) What predictions (hypothesis) did you make?

_____

_____

(d) How reliable and fair was your activity? _____

_____

(e) What safety features did you consider and what did you do to reduce the risks?

_____

_____

(f) Identify controls in the activity. _____

_____

(g) Identify any relevant dependent/independent/fixed variables in the activity.

_____

_____

(h) Draw a diagram of your apparatus.

(i) Record your results.

_____

_____

_____

_____

(j) What do you conclude from this activity?

_____

_____

(k) How reliable and fair was your activity?

_____

(l) What are two things you liked about this activity?

- _____

- _____

(m) What did you find difficult about this activity?

_____

_____

(n) If you were to do this activity again, what would you do differently?

_____

_____

Activity 15.3: Evaporation

(a) Date on which you carried out this activity. _____

(b) What question did you ask yourself?

_____

(c) What predictions (hypothesis) did you make? _____

_____

(d) How reliable and fair was your activity? _____

_____

(e) What safety features did you consider and what did you do to reduce the risks?

_____

_____

(f) Identify controls in the activity. _____

_____

(g) Identify any relevant dependent/independent/fixed variables in the activity.

_____

_____

(h) Draw a diagram of your apparatus.

(i) Record your results.

_____

_____

_____

_____

(j)   What do you conclude from this activity?

_____

_____

(k)   How reliable and fair was your activity?

_____

(l)   What are two things you liked about this activity?

• _____

• _____

(m)   What did you find difficult about this activity?

_____

_____

(n)   If you were to do this activity again, what would you do differently?

_____

_____

Activity 15.4: Distillation

(a)   Date on which you carried out this activity. _____

(b)   What question did you ask yourself?

_____

(c)   What predictions (hypothesis) did you make? _____

_____

(d)   How reliable and fair was your activity? _____

_____

(e)   What safety features did you consider and what did you do to reduce the risks?

_____

_____

(f)   Identify controls in the activity. _____

_____

(g)   Identify any relevant dependent/independent/fixed variables in the activity.

_____

_____

(h) Draw a diagram of your apparatus.

(i) Record your results.

_____

_____

_____

_____

(j) What do you conclude from this activity?

_____

_____

(k) How reliable and fair was your activity?

_____

(l) What are two things you liked about this activity?

  • _____

  • _____

(m) What did you find difficult about this activity?

_____

_____

(n) If you were to do this activity again, what would you do differently?

_____

_____

Activity 15.5: Chromatography

(a) Date on which you carried out this activity. _____

(b) What question did you ask yourself?

_____

(c) What predictions (hypothesis) did you make? _____

_____

(d) How reliable and fair was your activity? _____

_____

(e) What safety features did you consider and what did you do to reduce the risks?

_____

_____

(f) Identify controls in the activity. _____

_____

(g) Identify any relevant dependent/independent/fixed variables in the activity.

_____

_____

(h) Draw a diagram of your apparatus.

(i) Record your results.

_____

_____

_____

_____

(j) What do you conclude from this activity?

_____

_____

(k) What are two things you liked about this activity?

- _____

- _____

(l) What did you find difficult about this activity?

_____

_____

(m) If you were to do this activity again, what would you do differently?

_____

_____

Textbook question 15.12: Investigating Brand A crisps / Brand B crisps

(a) Date on which you carried out this activity _____

(b) In this activity what question did you ask yourself?

_____

(c) What predictions (hypothesis) did you make?

_____

_____

(d) How did you plan for this activity?

_____

_____

(e) How did you conduct this activity?

_____

_____

(f) How reliable and fair was your activity?

_____

_____

(g) What safety features did you consider and what did you do to reduce the risks?

_____

_____

(h) Identify controls in the activity.

_____

_____

(i) Identify any relevant dependent/independent/fixed variables in the activity.

_____

_____

(j) Draw a diagram of your apparatus.

(k) Record your results.

_____

_____

_____

_____

(l) What conclusion(s) did you reach?

_____

_____

_____

Reflection

(m) What did you learn about mass during physical and chemical changes?

_____

_____

(n) What are two things you liked about this activity?

• _____

• _____

(o) What did you find difficult about this activity?

_____

_____

(p) If you were to do this activity again, what would you do differently?

_____

_____

Self evaluation – Particles in solution

Now that you have completed this chapter, how well do you feel you understand each of the following (tick the relevant column)?

Topic	🙂	😐	🙁
Solutes			
Solvents			
Solutions			
The meanings of 'soluble', 'insoluble' and 'solubility'			
Dilute solutions			
Concentrated solutions			
Saturated solutions			
Mixtures			
Filtering			
Evaporation			
Distillation			
Chromatography			

Action plan: What I need to do to improve my learning _____

_____

_____

CHAPTER 16 BUILDING BLOCKS

Log onto **www.edcolearning.ie** to find the **Mind Map** for this chapter.

Homework questions

1   (a)   An element is a substance made up of _____ type of _____.

    (b)   Give three examples of elements.

       (i)   _____

       (ii)   _____

       (iii)   _____

2   Give an example of an element that is:

    (a)   A solid at room temperature _____

    (b)   A liquid at room temperature _____

    (c)   A gas at room temperature. _____

3   (a)   A molecule is made up of _____ or more _____ chemically combined.

    (b)   Give three examples of molecules.

       (i)   _____

       (ii)   _____

       (iii)   _____

4   State two differences between a mixture and a compound.

    (i)   _____

    (ii)   _____

5   Write down the names of the elements from which the following compounds are made.

Compound	Formula	Elements in compound
(a) Carbon dioxide	CO_2	
(b) Water	H_2O	
(c) Sodium chloride	$NaCl$	
(d) Hydrochloric acid	HCl	
(e) Iron sulfide	FeS	

6 An atom is made up of three types of particle. Name them.

(i) _____

(ii) _____

(iii) _____

7 Complete the table.

Particle	Charge	Location	Mass in atomic mass units
Proton	+1		
	0	In the nucleus	1
Electron			0

8 Define:

(a) Atomic number _____

(b) Mass number _____

9 The centre of an atom is called the _____ and the electrons are found

whizzing around in _____.

10 Write down the atomic number and mass number of the element sodium.

11
Na
23

Atomic number _____

Mass number _____

From this we can calculate sodium to have _____ protons,

_____ electrons and _____ neutrons.

11 Draw a simple atomic diagram of:

4
Be
9

12 Keywords. Write one short sentence using each of the following words:

(a) Atom _____

(b) Element _____

(c) Compound _____

(d) **Molecule** _____

(e) **Proton** _____

(f) **Neutron** _____

(g) **Electron** _____

(h) **Symbol** _____

Self evaluation – Building blocks

Now that you have completed this chapter, how well do you feel you understand each of the following (tick the relevant column)?

Topic	😊	😐	🙁
Elements			
Molecules			
Compounds			
Mixtures			
Properties of a compound and how they differ from the properties of the elements from which they are made			
Atoms			
Sub-atomic particles that make up an atom			
Protons			
Neutrons			
Electrons			
Atomic number of an element			
Mass number of an element			
Isotopes			

Action plan: What I need to do to improve my learning _____

_____

_____

Log onto **www.edcolearning.ie** to find the **Mind Map** for this chapter.

Homework questions

1   In the periodic table, the Russian chemist _____

arranged the elements according to their _____.

2   The periodic table contains groups and periods.

  (a)   What are groups?_____

  _____

  (b)   What are periods?_____

  _____

3   Match the group name with its group by drawing a line from one to the other:

Group 1	The noble gases
Group 2	The halogens
Group 7	The alkaline earth metals
Group 8	The alkali metals

4   The alkali metals include sodium and lithium. List three properties of alkali metals.

  (i)   _____

  (ii)   _____

  (iii)   _____

5   Look at the periodic table below. Which letters represent the following elements?

  (a)   A noble gas _____

  (b)   An element with one electron in its outer shell _____

  (c)   A halogen _____

  (d)   An element in period 3_____

  (e)   An element that reacts vigorously with water _____

6 Divide the following into elements (E) and compounds (C).

Element/compound	E or C	Element/compound	E or C
(a) Sodium chloride		(i) Oxygen	
(b) Sulfur		(j) Helium	
(c) Magnesium oxide		(k) Calcium	
(d) Lead		(l) Sulfuric acid	
(e) Water		(m) Sulfur dioxide	
(f) Methane		(n) Carbon monoxide	
(g) Propane		(o) Chlorine	
(h) Carbon dioxide			

7 (a) Refer to Figures 17.1 and 17.2 in the textbook. Complete this table to show that you understand how the periodic table is arranged.

Element	Symbol	Period	Group	Metal	Non-metal
Carbon					
	H				
		2	3		
Barium					
	He				

(b) In your group, complete the following table using the periodic table.

Element	Symbol	Period	Group	Metal	Non-metal
Hydrogen	H	1			
Carbon	C	4			
Nitrogen					
Oxygen					
Sulfur					
Chlorine					

8 **Keywords.** Write one short sentence using each of the following words:

(a) **Periodic table** _____

(b) **Periods** _____

(c) **Groups** _____

(d) **Alkali** _____

(e) **Halogens** _____

(f) Noble gases _____

(g) Ions _____

(h) Chemical formula _____

Self evaluation – The chemist's compass – the periodic table

Now that you have completed this chapter, how well do you feel you understand each of the following (tick the relevant column)?

Topic	🙂	😐	🙁
The periodic table and its arrangement			
Grouping of particular elements in the periodic table			
Names of the groups in the periodic table			
How and why elements react to achieve a full outer shell of electrons			
Number of electrons in the different shells			
Ions			
Ionic bonds			
Covalent bonds			
Metal + non-metal = compound			
The meaning of a chemical formula			
Predicting the ratio of atoms in compounds using the periodic table			

Action plan: What I need to do to improve my learning _____

_____

_____

Log onto **www.edcolearning.ie** to find the **Mind Map** for this chapter.

Homework questions

1 The following diagram summarises the properties of metals.

C

B

D

Metals

A

E

Malleable   Sonorous

Ductile

Fill in the missing properties A–E.

A _____

B _____

C _____

D _____

E _____

2 Match the metals from the list (a)–(g) with the correct descriptions.

(a) Lead

(b) Magnesium

(c) Sodium

(d) Mercury

(e) Aluminium

(f) Copper

(g) Gold

Description	Metal
The only metal that is liquid at room temperature	
Ladders are often made of this	
This metal is used in electric wiring	
This metal must be stored under oil	
Jewellery is often made of this	

3 (a) Mercury is an unusual metal. In what way is it unusual?

_____

(b) In what way do alkali metals differ from other metals?

_____

4 (a) What is an alloy?

_____

(b) Give two examples of alloys.

• _____

• _____

(c) Complete the first column of the table with the names of the alloys. One has been done for you.

Alloy	Use	Composition
(i)	Musical instruments, ornaments	Copper and zinc
(ii)	Statues	Copper and tin
(iii)	Soldering	Lead and tin
(iv)	Building reinforcement	Iron and carbon
(v)	Knives, sinks, etc.	Iron, chromium and nickel
Alico	Powerful magnets	Aluminium, nickel and cobalt

5 **Keywords.** Write one short sentence using each of the following words:

(a) **Physical properties** _____

_____

_____

(b) **Melting point** _____

_____

_____

(c) **Boiling point** _____

_____

_____

(d) **Conductivity** _____

_____

_____

(e) **Density** _____

_____

_____

(f) **Alloy** _____

_____

_____

Activities – Investigating properties of metals

Activity 18.1: Melting point

(a) Date on which you carried out this activity _____

(b) What question did you ask yourself?

_____

(c) What predictions (hypothesis) did you make?

_____

_____

(d) How reliable and fair was your activity?

_____

_____

(e) What safety features did you consider and what did you do to reduce the risks?

_____

_____

(f) Identify controls in the activity.

_____

_____

(g) Identify any relevant dependent/independent/fixed variables in the activity.

_____

_____

(h) Draw a diagram of your apparatus.

(i) Record your results.

_____

_____

(j) What do you conclude from this activity?

_____

_____

(k) What are two things you liked about this activity?

• _____

_____

• _____

_____

(l) What did you find difficult about this activity?

_____

_____

(m) If you were to do this activity again, what would you do differently?

_____

_____

Activity 18.2: Conduction of heat

(a) Date on which you carried out this activity _____

(b) What question did you ask yourself?

_____

(c) What predictions (hypothesis) did you make?

_____

_____

(d) How reliable and fair was your activity?

_____

_____

(e) What safety features did you consider and what did you do to reduce the risks?

_____

_____

(f)   Identify controls in the activity.

_____

_____

(g)   Identify any relevant dependent/independent/fixed variables in the activity.

_____

_____

(h)   Draw a diagram of your apparatus.

(i)   Record your results.

_____

_____

(j)   What do you conclude from this activity?

_____

_____

(k)   What are two things you liked about this activity?

•   _____

_____

•   _____

_____

(l)   What did you find difficult about this activity?

_____

_____

(m) If you were to do this activity again, what would you do differently?

_____

_____

Activity 18.3: Conduction of electricity

(a) Date on which you carried out this activity _____

(b) What question did you ask yourself?

_____

(c) What predictions (hypothesis) did you make?

_____

_____

(d) How reliable and fair was your activity?

_____

_____

(e) What safety features did you consider and what did you do to reduce the risks?

_____

_____

(f) Identify controls in the activity.

_____

_____

(g) Identify any relevant dependent/independent/fixed variables in the activity.

_____

_____

(h) Draw a diagram of your apparatus.

(i) Record your results.

_____

_____

(j) What do you conclude from this activity?

_____

_____

(k) What are two things you liked about this activity?

• _____

_____

• _____

_____

(l) What did you find difficult about this activity?

_____

_____

(m) If you were to do this activity again, what would you do differently?

_____

_____

Questions on the activities

6

Melting point

(a) Do any of the metals melt?

_____

(b) What can you say about the melting point of metals?

_____

Conductors of heat

(c) What do you see happening?

_____

(d) Can you tell which metal is the best conductor of heat?

_____

Conductors of electricity

(e) What happens each time you place a metal across the gap?

_____

(f) Are metals good conductors of electricity?

_____

Activity 18.4: Which materials are good conductors or insulators of electricity?

(a) Date on which you carried out this activity _____

(b) In this activity what question did you ask yourself?

_____

(c) What predictions (hypothesis) did you make?

_____

_____

(d) How did you plan for this activity?

_____

(e) How did you conduct this activity?

_____

_____

(f) Draw a diagram of your apparatus.

(g) How reliable and fair was your activity?

_____

_____

(h) What safety features did you consider and what did you do to reduce the risks?

_____

_____

(i) Identify controls in the activity.

_____

_____

(j)   Identify any relevant dependent/independent/fixed variables in the activity.

_____

_____

(k)   Record your results.

Material	Bulb lights	Insulator	Conductor
Wood	No	✓	
Copper			
Lead			
Coal			
Plastic			
Paper			

(l)   What conclusion(s) did you reach?

_____

_____

Reflection

(m) What are two things you liked about this activity?

•   _____

_____

•   _____

_____

(n)   What did you find difficult about this activity?

_____

_____

(o)   What did you learn from this activity?

_____

_____

(p)   If you were to do this activity again, what would you do differently?

_____

_____

Self evaluation – Metals and non-metals – properties and uses

Now that you have completed this chapter, how well do you feel you understand each of the following (tick the relevant column)?

Topic	🙂	😐	🙁
Properties of metals			
Metals as conductors of electricity and heat			
Malleability and ductility of metals			
Properties of non-metals			
Alloys			
Reactive metals			
Unreactive metals			

Action plan: What I need to do to improve my learning _____

_____

_____

MATERIALS SCIENCE –
FIT FOR PURPOSE

📄 Log onto **www.edcolearning.ie** to find the **Mind Map** for this chapter.

Homework questions

1 Plastics are _____ materials. Most plastics are made from _____.

This substance is separated into fractions by _____.

2 (a) Plastic bags stretch and melt easily. Does this indicate that the forces between the polymer chains are strong or weak?

_____

(b) A label on a plastic dustbin says 'No Hot Ashes'. Why, do you think, is this warning given?

_____

(c) What is the disadvantage of burning plastics to dispose of them?

_____

(d) What is the disadvantage of burying plastics to dispose of them?

_____

3 Some plastics are non-biodegradable. Explain the term 'non-biodegradable'.

_____

4 Give one advantage of:

(a) PVC windows in place of wooden windows_____

(b) Polystyrene cups in place of ceramic cups_____

(c) PVC guttering in place of metal guttering_____

(d) Moulded plastic seats in place of wooden seats_____

(e) Velcro fasteners in place of buttons_____.

5 Briefly outline two environmental disadvantages of plastics.

(i) _____

(ii) _____

6 List three advantages of manufacturing items from plastic instead of traditional materials.

(i) _____

(ii) _____

(iii) _____

7 Name two commonly used plastics.

(i) _____

(ii) _____

8 What particular property makes plastic suitable for use in:

(a) Light switches? _____

(b) Hot drinks containers? _____

(c) Spectacle lenses? _____

(d) Contact lenses? _____

(e) Underground pipes? _____

9 Each group of students must have a rubber band. Do the following:

(a) Make a sketch of how the particles are arranged in the unstretched rubber band.

(b) Predict what will happen to the **thickness** of the rubber band as it is stretched.

_____

_____

(c) Make a sketch of how the particles are arranged in the stretched rubber band.

(d) What do you think will happen to the stretchy bonds between the particles if the rubber band is stretched too far?

_____

_____

10 **Keywords.** Write one short sentence using each of the following words:

(a) Classify _____

(b) Natural _____

(c) Synthetic _____

(d) Tensile strength _____

(e) Compressive strength _____

(f) Elasticity _____

(g) Composites _____

(h) Ceramics _____

(i) Nanotechnology _____

Activity 19.1: Which paper has the greatest tearing strength?

(a) Date on which you carried out this activity _____

(b) In this activity what question did you ask yourself?

_____

(c) What predictions (hypothesis) did you make?

_____

_____

(d) How reliable and fair was your activity?

_____

_____

(e) What safety features did you consider and what did you do to reduce the risks?

_____

_____

(f) Identify controls in the activity.

_____

_____

(g) Identify any relevant dependent/independent/fixed variables in the activity.

_____

_____

(h) Draw a diagram of your apparatus.

(i) Record your results in this table.

Type of paper	Number of marbles	Mass of marbles (g)
Kitchen paper		
Napkin		
Tissue		
Newspaper		
Photocopying paper		

(j) What did you learn about the strength of paper?

_____

_____

Reflection

(k) What are two things you liked about this activity?

• _____

• _____

(l) What did you find difficult about this activity? _____

_____

(m) If you were to do this activity again, what would you do differently?

_____

_____

Self evaluation – Materials science – fit for purpose

Now that you have completed this chapter, how well do you feel you understand each of the following (tick the relevant column)?

Topic	😊	😐	🙁
Materials			
Properties of materials			
What determines the uses of a material			
Strength			
Hardness			
The definition of a 'stiff material'			
Elasticity			
Good conductors of heat and electricity			
Plastics			
How monomers join together to form polymers			
Bio-degradability of plastics			
Bioplastics			
Composites			
Ceramics			
Nanotechnology			

Action plan: What I need to do to improve my learning _____

_____

_____

CHAPTER 20 RATES OF REACTIONS

Log onto **www.edcolearning.ie** to find the **Mind Map** for this chapter.

Homework questions

1 Particles can react only if they _____ with enough _____ for the reaction to take place. There are four factors that can change the rate of a reaction: temperature, _____, surface area and a suitable _____.

2 **Temperature**
Increasing the temperature will cause the particles to have more _____. They will therefore move _____, which causes them to _____ faster. This means there is an _____ rate of reaction.

3 **Concentration**
Increasing the concentration of reactants simply means there are more _____, which means more _____ and therefore increased _____ of _____.

4 **Surface area**
Using powdered reactants instead of a lump means the _____ _____ is increased, which means more reactants are exposed and more _____, therefore an _____ rate of reaction.

5 **Rate of reactions**
Use of a catalyst causes a _____ in activation energy.
This makes it easier for the _____ to react so there is an _____ in the _____.

6 The graph shows an energy profile diagram.

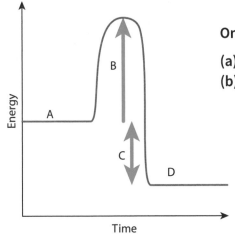

On the graph:
(a) Label A, B, C and D with the relevant words.
(b) Show what happens when the reaction is catalysed.

7 **Keywords.** Write one short sentence using each of the following words:

(a) Collide _____

(b) Concentration _____

(c) Temperature _____

(d) Surface area _____

(e) Catalyst _____

(f) Activation energy _____

Activity 20.1: **What factors increase the rate at which a dissolvable tablet dissolves in water?**

(a) Date on which you carried out this activity _____

(b) In this activity what question did you ask yourself?

_____

(c) What predictions (hypothesis) did you make?

_____

_____

(d) How reliable and fair was your activity?

_____

_____

(e) What safety features did you consider and what did you do to reduce the risks?

_____

_____

(f) Identify controls in the activity.

_____

_____

(g) Identify any relevant dependent/independent/fixed variables in the activity.

_____

_____

(h) Draw a diagram of your apparatus.

(i) Record your results in this table.

Conical flask	Temperature (°C)	Particle size	Time (s)
A			
B			
C			
D			
E			

(j) What conclusion can you make about the factors that affect the rate of a reaction?

_____

_____

Reflection

(k) What are two things you liked about this activity?

• _____

• _____

(l) What did you find difficult about this activity?

_____

_____

(m) If you were to do this activity again, what would you do differently?

_____

_____

Activity 20.2: What is the effect of increasing surface area on the rate of production of carbon dioxide?

(a) Date on which you carried out this activity _____

(b) In this activity what question did you ask yourself?

_____

(c) What predictions (hypothesis) did you make?

_____

_____

(d) How reliable and fair was your activity?

_____

_____

(e) What safety features did you consider and what did you do to reduce the risks?

_____

_____

(f) Identify controls in the activity.

_____

_____

(g) Identify any relevant dependent/independent/fixed variables in the activity.

_____

_____

(h) Draw a diagram of your apparatus.

(i) Record your results in this table.

Time (s)	Marble chips (5 mm)		Marble chips (10 mm)	
	Mass (g)	Loss in mass	Mass (g)	Loss in mass
0				
30				
60				
90				
120				
150				
180				

(j) (20.2) Which marble chips have the larger surface area?

_____

(k) **(20.3)** Why is it important to keep all other factors in the activity the same?

_____

_____

(l) **(20.4)** Plot both sets of results on a graph. Put loss of mass (mass of gas given off) on the *y*-axis and time on the *x*-axis.

(m) **(20.5)** Which size of marble chips reacts faster?

_____

(n) What happens to the rate of reaction as we increase the surface area?

_____

_____

Reflection

(o) What are two things you liked about this activity?

* _____

* _____

(p) What did you find difficult about this activity?

_____

_____

(q) If you were to do this activity again, what would you do differently?

_____

_____

✏ Activity 20.3: What is the effect of concentration on rate of reaction?

(a) Date on which you carried out this activity _____

(b) In this activity what question did you ask yourself?

_____

(c) What predictions (hypothesis) did you make?

_____

_____

(d) How reliable and fair was your activity?

_____

_____

(e) What safety features did you consider and what did you do to reduce the risks?

_____

_____

(f) Identify controls in the activity.

_____

_____

(g) Identify any relevant dependent/independent/fixed variables in the activity.

_____

_____

(h) Draw a diagram of your apparatus.

(i) Record your results in this table.

Acid (cm³)	Water (cm³)	Time to collect 20 cm³ of carbon dioxide (s)
10	40	
20	30	
30	20	
40	10	
50	0	

(j)   What happens to the rate of reaction as you increase the concentration of the acid?

_____

_____

Reflection

(k)   What are two things you liked about this activity?

•   _____

•   _____

(l)   What did you find difficult about this activity?

_____

_____

(m) If you were to do this activity again, what would you do differently?

_____

_____

Activity 20.4: What is the effect of a catalyst on the rate of a chemical reaction?

(a)   Date on which you carried out this activity _____

(b)   In this activity what question did you ask yourself?

_____

(c)   What predictions (hypothesis) did you make?

_____

_____

(d)   How reliable and fair was your activity?

_____

_____

(e)   What safety features did you consider and what did you do to reduce the risks?

_____

_____

(f)   Identify controls in the activity.

_____

_____

(g) Identify any relevant dependent/independent/fixed variables in the activity.

_____

_____

(h) Draw a diagram of your apparatus.

(i) Record your results.

_____

_____

(j) Did bubbles form in Test tube A?

_____

(k) What happened as soon as you added the catalyst manganese dioxide?

_____

_____

(l) Did the glowing splint relight in each test tube?

_____

(m) Which test tube showed the greater rate of reaction?

_____

(n) How did you judge the rate of reaction?

_____

_____

Reflection

(o) What are two things you liked about this activity?

• _____

• _____

(p) What did you find difficult about this activity? _____

_____

(q) If you were to do this activity again, what would you do differently? _____

_____

Activity 20.5: What is the effect of light intensity on photosynthesis?

(a) Date on which you carried out this activity _____

(b) In this activity what question did you ask yourself?

_____

(c) What predictions (hypothesis) did you make?

_____

_____

(d) How reliable and fair was your activity?

_____

_____

(e) What safety features did you consider and what did you do to reduce the risks?

_____

_____

(f) Identify controls in the activity.

_____

_____

(g) Identify any relevant dependent/independent/fixed variables in the activity.

_____

_____

(h) Draw a diagram of your apparatus.

(i) Record your results in this table.

Distance of light	Number of bubbles in 1 minute
10 cm	
20 cm	
30 cm	
40 cm	
50 cm	

(j) How was the number of bubbles of oxygen affected by moving the light away from the plant?

_____

(k) What would happen to the bubbles if the apparatus were covered with a black sack?

_____

(l) Outline a test for the oxygen gas produced.

_____

Reflection

(m) What are two things you liked about this activity?

- _____

- _____

(n) What did you find difficult about this activity? _____

_____

(o) If you were to do this activity again, what would you do differently? _____

_____

Self evaluation – Rates of reactions

Now that you have completed this chapter, how well do you feel you understand each of the following (tick the relevant column)?

Topic	🙂	😐	☹
What the rate of a chemical reaction measures			
What the rate of a chemical reaction depends on			
How the rate of reaction can be increased			
How the rate of reaction can be affected			
Activation energy			
How a catalyst works			

Action plan: What I need to do to improve my learning _____

_____

_____

CHAPTER 21 ACIDS AND BASES

 Log onto **www.edcolearning.ie** to find the **Mind Map** for this chapter.

Homework questions

1 (a) Lemon juice is a common everyday acid. Name two other household acids.

(i) _____

(ii) _____

(b) Name one acid found in the lab.

_____

2 Name parts A, B and C in the following diagram.

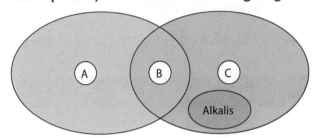

A _____

B _____

C _____

3 Litmus is an _____ which is coloured _____ in acids and in _____ bases.

If blue litmus stays blue and red litmus stays red, then the substance is said to be _____.

Litmus does not tell us the _____ of the solution.

4 A group of students tests a variety of substances using red litmus paper and blue litmus paper. They do this to determine whether the substances are acidic, basic or neutral.

Use the table below to predict their results.

Substance tested	Mixture	Acidic, basic or neutral
Vinegar	Red litmus stays red Blue litmus changes to red	Acidic
Washing-up liquid	(a) Red litmus: Blue litmus:	(b)
Lemon juice	(c) Red litmus: Blue litmus:	(d)
Water	(e) Red litmus: Blue litmus:	Neutral

5 **Keywords.** Write one short sentence using each of the following words:

(a) Acid _____

(b) Base _____

(c) Alkali _____

(d) Neutral _____

(e) Litmus paper _____

(f) Universal indicator _____

(g) pH scale _____

(h) Titration _____

(i) Neutralisation _____

Activity 21.1: **What household substances are acids, bases or neutral?**

Record your results in the grid, ticking the relevant column for whether the substance is an acid, a base or is neutral.

Substances being tested	Acidic	Basic	Neutral

Activity 21.2: **What is the pH of a variety of household substances?**

Record your results by drawing a number line from 0 to 14 for the pH scale and marking on it the various household products you tested.

Activity 21.3: How do you make your own indicator using red cabbage?

(a) Date on which you carried out this activity. _____

(b) In this activity what question did you ask yourself?

_____

(c) What predictions (hypothesis) did you make? _____

_____

(d) How reliable and fair was your activity? _____

_____

(e) What safety features did you consider and what did you do to reduce the risks?

_____

_____

(f) Identify controls in the activity when you were testing different substances with your indicator.

_____

_____

(g) Identify any relevant dependent/independent/fixed variables in the activity when testing different substances.

_____

_____

(h) Draw a diagram of your apparatus.

(i) Record your results in this table.

Substance tested	Name of substance	Indicator colour
Acidic substance		
Neutral substance		
Alkaline substance		

(j) What conclusion did you reach about using red-cabbage indicator?

_____

Reflection

(k) What are two things you liked about this activity?

• _____

• _____

(l) What did you find difficult about this activity? _____

_____

(m) If you were to do this activity again, what would you do differently?

_____

_____

Activity 21.4: What happens when calcium reacts with hydrochloric acid?

(a) Date on which you carried out this activity. _____

(b) In this activity what question did you ask yourself?

_____

(c) What predictions (hypothesis) did you make? _____

_____

(d) How reliable and fair was your activity? _____

_____

(e) What safety features did you consider and what did you do to reduce the risks?

_____

_____

(f) Identify controls in the activity when you were testing different substances with your indicator.

_____

_____

(g) Identify any relevant dependent/independent/fixed variables in the activity when testing different substances.

_____

_____

(h) Draw a diagram of your apparatus.

(i) Record your results. _____

_____

(j) What conclusions did you reach? _____

_____

Reflection

(k) What are two things you liked about this activity?

• _____

• _____

(l) What did you find difficult about this activity? _____

_____

(m) If you were to do this activity again, what would you do differently?

_____

Activity 21.5: How do you titrate hydrochloric acid (HCl) against sodium hydroxide (NaOH) and prepare a sample of sodium chloride (NaCl)?

(a) Date on which you carried out this activity _____

(b) In this activity what question did you ask yourself?

_____

(c) What predictions (hypothesis) did you make? _____

_____

(d) How reliable and fair was your activity? _____

_____

(e) What safety features did you consider and what did you do to reduce the risks?

_____

_____

(f) Identify controls in the activity. _____

_____

(g) Identify any relevant dependent/independent/fixed variables in the activity.

_____

_____

(h) Draw a diagram of your apparatus.

(i)

Titration	Volume of acid added to change indicator colour	Average volume of acid needed to change indicator colour
Titration 1		
Titration 2		

(j) What conclusions did you reach? _____

_____

Reflection

(k) What are two things you liked about this activity?

• _____

• _____

(l) What did you find difficult about this activity? _____

_____

(m) If you were to do this activity again, what would you do differently?

_____

_____

Activity 21.6: Which brand of indigestion tablet is the most effective at neutralising an acid?

(a) Date on which you carried out this activity _____

(b) In this activity what question did you ask yourself?

_____

(c) What predictions (hypothesis) did you make? _____

_____

(d) How reliable and fair was your activity? _____

_____

(e) What safety features did you consider and what did you do to reduce the risks?

_____

_____

(f) Identify controls in the activity. _____

_____

(g) Identify any relevant dependent/independent/fixed variables in the activity.

_____

_____

(h) Draw a diagram of your apparatus.

(i) Record your results in the table below.

Brand	Volume of HCl neutralised by table (cm³)		
	Titre 1	Titre 2	Average

(j)   Draw a bar chart or line graph showing the results for each brand of tablet.

(k)   What conclusion(s) did you reach? _____

_____

Reflection

(l)   What are two things you liked about this activity?

•   _____

•   _____

(m) What did you find difficult about this activity? _____

_____

(n)   If you were to do this activity again, what would you do differently?

_____

_____

Self evaluation – Acids and bases

Now that you have completed this chapter, how well do you feel you understand each of the following (tick the relevant column)?

Topic	😊	😐	😞
Acids			
The most common laboratory acids			
Bases			
Alkalis			
Reading a pH scale			
Acids reacting with bases			
Acids reacting with carbonates			
Acids reacting with metals			
Determining whether hydrogen gas is present			

Action plan: What I need to do to improve my learning _____

_____

_____

CHAPTER 22

ENERGY TRANSFER IN CHEMICAL REACTIONS

Log onto **www.edcolearning.ie** to find the **Mind Map** for this chapter.

Homework questions

1 What type of chemical reaction absorbs energy and requires energy for a reaction to occur?

_____

2 What type of reaction releases energy and does not require energy to occur?

_____

3 Tick the exothermic chemical reactions in the following list:

(a) Freezing water ☐

(b) Burning a piece of wood ☐

(c) Photosynthesis ☐

4 Photosynthesis is an endothermic chemical reaction. Explain why. _____

_____

5 Where will the products be in relation to the reactants in an endothermic energy diagram?

_____

6 What symbol is used to represent an energy change in a chemical reaction?

_____

7 **Keywords.** Write one short sentence using each of the following words:

(a) Exothermic _____

_____

(b) Endothermic _____

_____

(c) Bond energy _____

_____

(d) Activation energy _____

_____

(e) Energy profile diagram _____

_____

Activity 22.1: **What energy changes occur in chemical reactions?**

(a) Date on which you carried out this activity _____

(b) In this activity what question did you ask yourself?

_____

(c) What predictions (hypothesis) did you make? _____

_____

(d) How reliable and fair was your activity? _____

_____

(e) What safety features did you consider and what did you do to reduce the risks?

_____

(f) Identify controls in the activity. _____

_____

(g) Identify any relevant dependent/independent/fixed variables in the activity.

_____

(h) Draw a diagram of your apparatus.

(i) Record your results in the grid below.

Reaction	Initial °C (temperature)	Final °C (temperature)	Endothermic or exothermic
A			
B			
C			
D			

_____

_____

(j) What conclusions did you reach? _____

_____

Reflection

(k) What are two things you liked about this activity?

- _____

_____

- _____

_____

(l) What did you find difficult about this activity? _____

_____

(m) If you were to do this activity again, what would you do differently?

_____

Self evaluation – Energy transfer in chemical reactions

Now that you have completed this chapter, how well do you feel you understand each of the following (tick the relevant column)?

Topic	☺	😐	☹
Exothermic reactions			
Endothermic reactions			
The process for breaking bonds			
The process for forming bonds			
Bond energy			
Energy profile diagrams			
Activation energy			

Action plan: What I need to do to improve my learning _____

_____

_____

CHAPTER 23

ENVIRONMENTAL IMPACT OF MATERIALS

Log onto **www.edcolearning.ie** to find the **Mind Map** for this chapter.

Homework questions

1 Tick the more sustainable choice in each of the following situations:

    (a)   When I bring my lunch to school, I bring:

        (i)   A homemade sandwich   ☐

        (ii) A pre-packaged bought sandwich.   ☐

    (b)   I live close to school. I:

        (i)   Walk or cycle to school   ☐

        (ii) Get my parents to drive me to school.   ☐

    (c)   In my garden I:

        (i)   Spray herbicide to keep weeds down   ☐

        (ii) Pull the weeds by hand.   ☐

    (d)   When I buy my own car, I want:

        (i)   The biggest, fastest car   ☐

        (ii) A hybrid or fuel-efficient vehicle.   ☐

    (e)   I need to buy a school copy, so I:

        (i)   Buy whatever paper looks best   ☐

        (ii) Buy recycled paper.   ☐

2 Complete the life cycle of a product in the diagram.

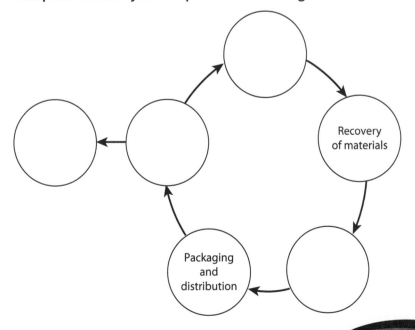

3   Read the following ideas and decide if you think it:

(a)   Will never happen

(b)   Could happen

(c)   Will happen in the next 30 years.

Mark each sentence a, b or c.

(i)   All cars will be electric. _____

(ii)   Alternative energy will be more important than oil. _____

(iii)   All cans, paper and bags will be recycled. _____

(iv)   The climate will get worse. _____

(v)   People will always sunbathe. _____

(vi)   All the rainforests will disappear. _____

(vii)   The next generation will care more about the environment. _____

(viii)   People will destroy Earth. _____

4   **Keywords.**   Write one short sentence using each of the following words:

(a)   Environment _____

(b)   Extraction _____

(c)   Transportation _____

(d)   Manufacturing _____

(e)   Raw materials _____

(f)   Life cycle _____

(g)   Sustainable development _____

(h)   Electrolysis _____

(i)   Distribution _____

(j)   Recycling _____

(k)   Composting _____

✎ **Activity 23.1:** Can you extract copper metal from copper oxide using carbon?

(a) Date on which you carried out this activity _____

(b) In this activity what question did you ask yourself?

_____

(c) What predictions (hypothesis) did you make?

_____

_____

(d) How reliable and fair was your activity?

_____

_____

(e) What safety features did you consider and what did you do to reduce the risks?

_____

_____

(f) Identify controls in the activity.

_____

_____

(g) Identify any relevant dependent/independent/fixed variables in the activity.

_____

_____

(h) Draw a diagram of your apparatus.

(i) Record your results. _____

_____

(j) Did a reaction occur, and what is the colour of any metal produced or visible?

_____

(k) What conclusions did you reach?

_____

_____

Reflection

(l) What are two things you liked about this activity?

• _____

• _____

(m) What did you find difficult about this activity?

_____

_____

(n) If you were to do this activity again, what would you do differently?

_____

_____

Activity 23.2: How can we make old paper into new, reusable paper?

(a) Date on which you carried out this activity _____

(b) In this activity what question did you ask yourself?

_____

(c) What predictions (hypothesis) did you make?

_____

_____

(d) How reliable and fair was your activity?

_____

_____

(e) What safety features did you consider and what did you do to reduce the risks?

_____

_____

(f) Identify controls in the activity.

_____

_____

(g) Draw a diagram of your apparatus.

(h) Record your results.

_____

_____

(i) What conclusions did you reach?

_____

_____

Reflection

(j) What are two things you liked about this activity?

- _____

- _____

(k) What did you find difficult about this activity?

_____

_____

(l) If you were to do this activity again, what would you do differently?

_____

_____

Self evaluation – Environmental impact of materials

Now that you have completed this chapter, how well do you feel you understand each of the following (tick the relevant column)?

Topic	☺	😐	☹
Sustainable development			
Life cycle of a product			
Extraction of metal by chemical reduction using carbon or electrolysis			
The impact of extraction on the environment			
Energy used in manufacturing, packaging and distribution			
Making products from recycled materials			
Production of methane gas and how it can be used to generate electricity or as a source of fuel for boilers			
Composting			
Sustainable products			
Technical materials			
Biological materials			

Action plan: What I need to do to improve my learning _____

_____

_____

Peer Assessment

Date:__/__/__

_____   _____   _____
Your name   Name of lab partner   Title of work

Success Criteria	**How** did this piece of work achieve the success criteria?

Two excellent points	This could be improved by…
1	
2	

MAKING ACCURATE MEASUREMENTS

Log onto **www.edcolearning.ie** to find the **Mind Map** for this chapter.

Homework questions

1   Give three examples of where accurate measurements are needed in everyday life.

(i)   _____

(ii)   _____

(iii)   _____

2   What is one benefit of having an international system of units?

_____

_____

3   List five measurements that you have made and the units that you used.

Measurement	Unit

4   Convert:

(a)   52 cm to mm _____

(b)   5.2 cm to mm _____

(c)   0.52 cm to mm _____

5   Convert:

(a)   92 mm to cm _____

(b)   920 mm to cm _____

(c)   9.2 mm to cm _____

6   Convert:

(a)   63 km to m _____

(b)   6.3 km to m _____

(c)   0.63 km to m _____

7 How many seconds are there in 3 weeks?

There are 7 days in a week, therefore 3 weeks = _____ days

There are 24 hours in a day, therefore 3 weeks = _____ hours

There are 60 minutes in an hour, therefore 3 weeks = _____ minutes

There are 60 seconds in a minute, therefore 3 weeks = _____ seconds

8 Calculate the volume of a rectangular box with the following dimensions:

(a) Length 90 cm, width 60 cm, height 15 cm

_____

(b) Length 2 m, width 50 cm, height 12 cm

_____

(c) Length 2.4 m, width 1 m, height 8 cm

_____

(Note: Be careful: you must change the m to cm. Make sure that all the units are the same.)

9 Calculate the volume of a cube:

(a) With a side of length 25 cm _____

(b) With a side of length 0.5 m _____

(c) With a side of length 2 m _____

(Note: What units will you use here?)

10 **Keywords.** Write one short sentence using each of the following words:

(a) Length _____

(b) Units _____

(c) Opisometer _____

(d) Trundle wheel _____

(e) Vernier caliper _____

(f) Zero error _____

(g) Mass _____

(h) Balance _____

(i) Timer _____

(j) Meniscus _____

(k) Graduated cylinder _____

Activity 24.1: How can we measure without measuring instruments?

(a) Date on which you carried out this activity _____

(b) In this activity what question did you ask yourself?

_____

(c) What predictions (hypothesis) did you make?

_____

(d) How reliable and fair was your activity?

_____

(e) What safety features did you consider and what did you do to reduce the risks?

_____

(f) Record your results in the following table.

Item	Your group's measurements	Other group's measurements
Lunch box		
Goal posts		
Bicycle		

(g) What conclusion(s) did you reach?

_____

Reflection

(h) What are two things you liked about this activity?

• _____

• _____

(i) What did you find difficult about this activity?

_____

(j) If you were to do this activity again, what would you do differently?

_____

Activity 24.2: How can we measure the volume of an irregular shape?

(a) Date on which you carried out this activity _____

(b) In this activity what question did you ask yourself?

_____

(c) What predictions (hypothesis) did you make?

_____

(d) How reliable and fair was your activity?

_____

(e) What safety features did you consider and what did you do to reduce the risks?

_____

(f) Record your results:

Level of water before placing stone in overflow can: _____

Level of water after placing stone in overflow can: _____

Volume of stone: _____

_____

(g) Draw and label a simple diagram of the activity.

(h) What conclusion(s) did you reach? _____

(i) How did you make sure that the water was at the level of the spout?

_____

(j) How did you read the level of water in the graduated cylinder?

_____

(k) What did you do to avoid splashing when you placed the stone in the overflow can?

_____

Reflection

(l) What are two things you liked about this activity?

• _____

• _____

(m) What did you find difficult about this activity?

_____

(n) If you were to do this activity again, what would you do differently?

_____

Self evaluation – Making accurate measurements

Now that you have completed this chapter, how well do you feel you understand each of the following (tick the relevant column)?

Topic	🙂	😐	🙁
Why it is important to be accurate with measurement			
Why we need an international system of units			
Converting km to m and converting cm to mm			
Calculating the number of seconds in a week			
Measurement of length			
Measurement of mass			
Measurement of time			
Measurement of area			
Measurement of volume			

Action plan: **What I need to do to improve my learning** _____

_____

WHAT IS DENSITY AND WHY DO SOME THINGS FLOAT?

Log onto **www.edcolearning.ie** to find the **Mind Map** for this chapter.

Homework questions

1 Which feels heavier to carry: a school bag full of vegetables, or a school bag stuffed with tissue paper? Explain your answer.

_____

_____

2 Identical twins Emma and Naomi are going on holidays and are bringing identical clothes in identical suitcases. Emma is neat and packs her suitcase in a very tidy manner. Naomi is very sloppy and throws all her clothes into her suitcase.

(a) Will the packed suitcases have the same mass? Explain.

_____

_____

(b) Will the packed suitcases have the same density? Explain.

_____

_____

3 The density of water changes when the temperature of the water changes. At what temperature is water at its most dense?

_____

4 Tick the relevant box for whether each of the following statements is true or false:

	True	False
(a) Cork will sink in paraffin oil.	☐	☐
(b) Ice will sink in paraffin oil.	☐	☐
(c) Ice will sink in water.	☐	☐
(d) Paraffin oil will float on top of water.	☐	☐
(e) Gold will float on top of water.	☐	☐

5 Using a mathematical approach, explain what density is.

_____

_____

6 Write down the two sets of units that density can be measured in.

(i) _____   (ii) _____

7 Complete the following sentences:

(a) A solid will float in a liquid if the...

_____

(b) A liquid will float on top of another liquid if the liquid on top...

_____

8 A student noted that 100 cm³ of a liquid had a mass of 120 g. Calculate the density of this liquid. _____

_____

9 A substance has a density of 12 g cm⁻³. Calculate the mass of 10 cm³ of this substance.

_____

_____

10 The density of a stone is 4 g cm⁻³. Calculate the volume of this stone if it has a mass of 160 g.

_____

_____

11 A student measured the values of the volume for five different pieces of wood. Each piece of wood had its mass value written on it. She presented the data as shown in the table below.

Mass (g)	2	4	6	8	10
Volume (cm³)	2.5	5	7.5	10	12.5

Draw a graph with values of mass on the *y*-axis and values of volume on the *x*-axis.

(a) What do you notice about the shape of the graph?

_____

(b) Divide any mass value by its corresponding volume value. Do you notice any pattern?

_____

(c) What unit would you get when a mass value is divided by a volume value?

_____

12 A rectangular block has a length of 5 m, a width of 1.5 m and a height of 1.2 m. It has a mass of 36 000 kg.

(a) Calculate the density of the block. _____

(b) State the unit of density used here. _____

13 A rectangular block has a length of 42 cm, a width of 22 cm and a height of 6 cm. It has a mass of 22 176 g.

(a) Calculate the density of the block.

_____

(b) State the unit of density used here.

_____

14 A rectangular block has a length of 2.5 m, a width of 60 cm and a height of 30 cm. It has a mass of 1215 kg.

(a) Calculate the density of the block.

_____

(b) State the unit of density used here.

_____

(Hint: be careful with your units!)

15 A rectangular block has a length of 40 cm, a width of 28 cm and a height of 12 cm. It has a mass of 26.88 kg.

(a) Calculate the density of the block.

_____

(b) State the unit of density used here.

_____

(Hint: be careful with your units!)

16 A rectangular block has a length of 1.8 m, a width of 60 cm and a height of 15 cm. It has a mass of 648 000 g.

(a) Calculate the density of the block.

_____

(b) State the unit of density used here.

_____

(Hint: be careful with your units!)

17 Keywords. Write one short sentence using each of the following words:

(a) Density _____

(b) Flotation _____

(c) Mass_____

(d) Volume _____

(e) Overflow can _____

(f) g cm^{-3} _____

(g) kg m^{-3} _____

(h) Graph _____

Activity 25.1: What is the relationship between mass and volume?

(a) Date on which you carried out this activity _____

(b) In this activity what question did you ask yourself?

_____

(c) What predictions (hypothesis) did you make?

_____

(d) How reliable and fair was your activity?

_____

(e) What safety features did you consider and what did you do to reduce the risks?

_____

(f) Record your results of question 2 of the activity in the following table:

Value of mass (g)	Volume of the weights (cm³)
25	
50	
100	
200	
500	

(g) Draw a graph with mass values on the *y*-axis and volume values on the *x*-axis.

(h) Record the results of question 3 of the activity in the following table.

Material of object	Volume of object (cm³)

(i) What conclusion(s) did you reach?

_____

(j) Why did you choose cm³ as the unit for volume in this activity?

_____

Reflection

(k) What are two things you liked about this activity?

- _____

- _____

(l) What did you find difficult about this activity?

_____

(m) If you were to do this activity again, what would you do differently?

_____

Activity 25.2: Why do some objects float and other objects sink?

(a) Date on which you carried out this activity _____

(b) In this activity what question did you ask yourself?

_____

(c) What predictions (hypothesis) did you make?

_____

(d) How reliable and fair was your activity?

_____

(e) What safety features did you consider and what did you do to reduce the risks?

_____

(f) Record your results by ticking the correct column.

Item	Floats on water	Floats on oil
Ice cube		
Cork		
Brass weight		

(g) What did you observe when you poured the water on top of the oil in the third beaker?

_____

(h) What conclusion can you make from the observation recorded in question (g)?

_____

(i) What conclusions can you make from the results that you recorded in the table at (f)?

_____

Reflection

(j) What are two things you liked about this activity?

- _____

- _____

(k) What did you find difficult about this activity?

_____

_____

(l) If you were to do this activity again, what would you do differently?

_____

_____

Self evaluation – What is density and why do some things float?

Now that you have completed this chapter, how well do you feel you understand each of the following (tick the relevant column)?

Topic	🙂	😐	🙁
Meaning of density			
Units for density			
Calculation of density			
Calculation of mass			
Calculation of volume			
Flotation			

Action plan: What I need to do to improve my learning _____

_____

Log onto **www.edcolearning.ie** to find the **Mind Map** for this chapter.

Homework questions

1 There are different types of motion. Give two examples of:

(a) Objects that vibrate as they move:

(i) _____

(ii) _____

(b) Objects that move in a circular manner:

(i) _____

(ii) _____

(c) Objects that move in a straight line:

(i) _____

(ii) _____

2 Arrange the following in order 1–6, starting with the slowest (1) and ending with the fastest (6).

	Order (1–6, slowest to fastest speed)
A jet flying at its fastest speed	
A snail moving at its fastest speed	
A cyclist pedalling as fast as possible	
A person walking as fast as possible	
The speed at which light travels	
A racing car moving at its fastest speed	

3 Complete the following:

(a) Speed = _____ / _____

The unit for speed is _____

(b) Velocity = _____

The unit for velocity is _____

(c) Acceleration = _____ – _____ / time taken for the change in speed

The unit for acceleration is _____

4 Complete the following table by converting all the values given into metres.

Value	Value in metres
67 cm	
8 cm	
125 cm	
78.5 cm	
4 km	
2.57 km	
100 km	
200.7 km	

5 Calculate the speed of a car that travels 600 m in a time of 20 s.

6 Calculate the speed of a train that travels a distance of 8 km in a time of 2 min.

7 How much time does it take a car travelling at a speed of 36 ms^{-1} to travel a distance of 720 m?

8 Calculate the distance travelled by a person running at a speed of 5 ms^{-1} for 90 minutes.

9 A car is observed to be moving at a speed of 4 ms^{-1}. After 9 s the car is seen to be moving at a speed of 40 ms^{-1}. Calculate the acceleration of the car.

10 A train starts from rest in a station and after 2 min it is moving at a speed of 60 ms⁻¹. Calculate the acceleration of this train.

_____

_____

_____

11 A car was observed to be travelling at a speed of 35 ms⁻¹. After a time of 11 s the speed of the car had changed to 2 ms⁻¹. Calculate the acceleration.

_____

_____

_____

12 The graph below represents the motion of a car as recorded by a stationary student.

(a) How far was the car from the student at the start of the recording?

_____

(b) Calculate the average speed of the car between points A and B.

_____

(c) Calculate the average speed of the car between points B and C.

_____

(d) What aspect of the graph indicates that one speed is greater than the other?

_____

(e) What is the average speed of the car between points D and E?

_____

(f) Is there any difference between the motion from D to E and the motion from B to C?

_____

13 The graph below represents the motion of a cyclist.

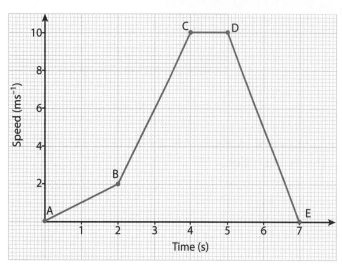

(a) Calculate the acceleration between points A and B. _____

(b) Calculate the acceleration between points C and D. _____

(c) Calculate the deceleration between points D and E. _____

(d) What is the value of the acceleration between points B and C? _____

14 Keywords. Write one short sentence using each of the following words:

(a) Speed _____

(b) Velocity _____

(c) Acceleration _____

✏ **Activity 26.1: What is the relationship between distance and time?**

(a) Date on which you carried out this activity _____

(b) In this activity what question did you ask yourself?

_____

(c) What predictions (hypothesis) did you make?

_____

(d) How reliable and fair was your activity?

_____

(e) What safety features did you consider and what did you do to reduce the risks?

_____

(f) Identify controls in the activity. (Possible answer: Make sure all students walk or run the same 50 m. Do not have some students running uphill and some downhill.)

_____

_____

(g) Identify any relevant dependent/independent/fixed variables in the activity.

_____

_____

(h) Record your results in the following table.

Distance (m)	Time to reach distance while walking (s)	Time to reach distance while running (s)
10		
20		
30		
40		
50		

(i) Draw a graph for the student walking (time on the *x*-axis, distance on the *y*-axis).

(j) Draw a graph for the student running (time on the *x*-axis, distance on the *y*-axis).

(k) How did you accurately mark out the distances?

_____

(l) How did you accurately measure the time values?

_____

(m) What are two things you liked about this activity?

• _____

• _____

(n) What did you find difficult about this activity?

_____

_____

(o) If you were to do this activity again, what would you do differently?

_____

_____

Activity 26.2: How can you identify acceleration?

(a) Date on which you carried out this activity _____

(b) In this activity, what question did you ask yourself?

_____

(c) What predictions (hypothesis) did you make?

_____

(d) How reliable and fair was your activity?

_____

(e) What safety features did you consider and what did you do to reduce the risks?

_____

(f) Identify any controls in the activity.

_____

(g) Compare the two graphs that you obtained with your data logging equipment and answer the following questions:

(i) Do the graphs have the same shape?

_____

(ii) How do the graphs differ?

_____

(iii) Which angle of tilt caused the greatest acceleration?

_____

Reflection

(h) **What are two things you liked about this activity?**

- _____

- _____

(i) **What did you find difficult about this activity?**

_____

_____

(j) **If you were to do this activity again, what would you do differently?**

_____

_____

Self evaluation – Measuring speed and acceleration

Now that you have completed this chapter, how well do you feel you understand each of the following (tick the relevant column)?

Topic	🙂	😐	🙁
Meaning of speed			
Meaning of velocity			
Meaning of acceleration			
Calculation of speed			
Calculation of velocity			
Calculation of acceleration			

Action plan: **What I need to do to improve my learning** _____

_____

FORCE, WORK, POWER AND PRESSURE

CHAPTER 27

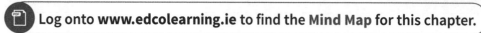

Log onto **www.edcolearning.ie** to find the **Mind Map** for this chapter.

Homework questions

1 Complete the table by writing either the word 'mass' or the word 'weight' in the right-hand column to match the left-hand side.

	Mass/weight
Measured in newtons	
The amount of matter in something	
Gets smaller as you rise upwards from ground level	
Does not have a direction	
Has a direction that acts towards Earth	
The pull of Earth on an object	
Remains the same	
Is measured in grams or kilograms	

2 What is the weight of an object of mass 8.5 kg? _____

_____

_____

3 Calculate the weight of an object of mass 400 g. _____

_____

_____

4

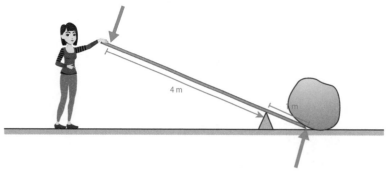

4 m

m

(a) If the student applied a force of 300 N on the bar, calculate the force applied to the

large rock. _____

_____

(b) If the student wants to apply a force of 1000 N to the large rock, what force must she apply to the bar? _____

_____

(c) If the 4 m length of bar was only 1 m long and the other 1 m length was changed to 20 cm, what force would be applied to the rock? Note that the total length of the bar is now 1 m and 20 cm long and the force applied to the bar is at 500 N.

_____

_____

● 5   A force of 500 N acts on an area of 25 m². Calculate the pressure. _____

_____

_____

● 6   Calculate the pressure on the ground if a person of weight 450 N were to balance themselves on one heel of a stiletto shoe. The area of the heel of the shoe is 1 cm².

_____

_____

● 7   Calculate the pressure on the ground of an elephant of weight 45 000 N standing on one foot. The area of the elephant's foot is 450 cm². _____

_____

● 8   A force of 70 N is being used to move an object a distance of 30 m. Calculate the work done.

_____

_____

● 9   Calculate the work done when a force of 25 N moves an object a distance of 60 cm.

_____

_____

● 10   A force of 10 N is being used to move an object a distance of 20 m in a time of 5 seconds. Calculate:

(a) The work done _____

(b) The value of average power _____

11   **Keywords.** Write one short sentence using each of the following words:

(a) Force _____

(b) Moment of a force _____

(c) Lever _____

(d) Work _____

(e) Pressure _____

(f) Power _____

(g) Extension _____

Activity 27.1: How can we see the relationship between weight and mass?

(a) Date on which you carried out this activity _____

(b) In this activity what question did you ask yourself?

_____

(c) What predictions (hypothesis) did you make?

_____

(d) How reliable and fair was your activity? _____

_____

(e) What safety features did you consider and what did you do to reduce the risks?

_____

_____

(f) Identify any controls in the activity.

_____

(g) Record your measurements.

Weight (N)	Mass

(h) Draw a graph with mass values on the *x*-axis and weight values on the *y*-axis.

(i)   Did you measure the mass in kilograms or in grams?

_____

(j)   Why did you choose this unit of measurement?

_____

Reflection

(k)   What are two things you liked about this activity?

•   _____

•   _____

(l)   What did you find difficult about this activity?

_____

_____

(m) If you were to do this activity again, what would you do differently?

_____

_____

Activity 27.2:   What is the relationship between the extension of a spring and the applied force?

(a)   Date on which you carried out this activity _____

(b)   In this activity what question did you ask yourself?

_____

(c)   What predictions (hypothesis) did you make? _____

_____

(d)   How reliable and fair was your activity?

_____

(e)   What safety features did you consider and what did you do to reduce the risks?

_____

(f)   Identify controls in the activity.

_____

(g)   Identify any relevant dependent/independent/fixed variables in the activity.

_____

(h) Record your results in the following table.

Value of weight (force) (N)	Value of extension (cm)

(i) Create a graph of your results.

(j) Draw and label a simple diagram of your equipment.

(k) What conclusion(s) did you reach?

(l) How did you change the value of the force used to extend the spring?

_____

_____

(m) How did you measure the extension of the spring? _____

_____

(n) What was the benefit of having a pointer on one side of the holder that was used for the weights? _____

_____

Reflection

(o) What are two things you liked about this activity?

- _____

- _____

(p) What did you find difficult about this activity? _____

_____

(q) If you were to do this activity again, what would you do differently?

_____

_____

Activity 27.3: How can we demonstrate the moment of a force?

(a) Date on which you carried out this activity _____

(b) In this activity what question did you ask yourself?

_____

(c) What predictions (hypothesis) did you make? _____

_____

(d) How reliable and fair was your activity? _____

_____

(e) What safety features did you consider and what did you do to reduce the risks?

_____

_____

(f) Identify any controls in the activity.

_____

(g) Record your results in the following table.

Position from hinge (cm)	Force described in words
20	
40	
60	
80	

(h) What conclusion(s) did you reach? _____

_____

_____

Reflection

(i) What are two things you liked about this activity?

- _____

- _____

(j) What did you find difficult about this activity? _____

_____

(k) If you were to do this activity again, what would you do differently?

_____

_____

Self evaluation – Force, work, power and pressure

Now that you have completed this chapter, how well do you feel you understand each of the following (tick the relevant column)?

Topic	😊	😐	🙁
Force			
Lever			
Moment of force			
Pressure			
Work			
Power			
Weight			
Mass			
Elastic limit			

Action plan: What I need to do to improve my learning _____

_____

CHAPTER 28 ENERGY

Log onto www.edcolearning.ie to find the **Mind Map** for this chapter.

Homework questions

1   Draw a line between each type of energy on the left and its explanation on the right.

Moving objects have this   Chemical energy

The food we eat contains this   Solar energy

Is released by splitting atoms   Kinetic energy

Comes from the Sun   Sound energy

Vibrating guitar strings give this   Heat energy

The mercury level rises in a thermometer because of this   Nuclear energy

2   The table below has a list of electrical devices you might have at home. They all change electrical energy to other forms of energy. Complete the table by filling in the other form of energy.

Electrical energy from...	Type of energy converted into...
Toaster	
Bulb	
Television	
Vacuum cleaner	
Music speaker	
Electric carving knife	
Electric iron	

3   Energy can make things move. What kind of energy causes each of the following types of movement?

(a)   The hands of a clock _____

(b)   Steam rising in a kettle _____

(c)   Hair dryer blowing out hot air _____

(d)   People walking _____

(e)   Sound from a violin _____

4   Suggest two things that could be done at home to reduce the waste of useful energy.

(i)   _____

(ii) _____

5 Suggest two things that could be done at school to reduce the waste of useful energy.

(i) _____

(ii) _____

6 Suggest two things that car drivers could do to reduce the waste of useful energy.

(i) _____

(ii) _____

7 Answer the following questions on solar water heaters.

(a) What form of energy do we get from the Sun? _____

(b) What material is used for the pipes in a solar water heater? _____

(c) What energy change occurs in a solar water heater? _____

(d) Give two uses for the hot water from solar water heaters.

(i) _____

(ii) _____

8 After eating breakfast you cycle to school and your dynamo provides the electricity to light up the bicycle lamp. Fill in the missing forms of energy below.

chemical energy → _____ energy → _____ energy → _____ energy

9 What causes the magnet to rotate inside the dynamo?

_____

_____

10 Give two examples of energy dissipation as you pedal your bicycle.

(i) _____

(ii) _____

11 Sound travels through the air at about 340 m s^{-1}. How far would sound travel in air for a time of:

(a) 2 seconds? _____

(b) 10 seconds? _____

(c) 1 minute? _____

(d) 5 minutes? _____

12 Sound is caused by a vibration. What form of energy is associated with a vibration?

_____

13 Things such as military jets, missiles and rockets can travel faster than the speed of sound in air. Research the words used to describe something travelling at a speed faster than the speed of sound in air.

_____

_____

14

Using the information in the diagram, compare the electrical energy that is put into each lamp with the amount of light energy produced.

_____

_____

Calculate the percentage of light energy produced in each case.

_____

_____

15 Keywords. Write one short sentence using each of the following words:

(a) Energy _____

(b) Energy conservation _____

(c) Energy dissipation _____

(d) Energy change _____

(e) Energy efficiency _____

Activity 28.1: How can we show that sound has energy?

(a) Date on which you carried out this activity _____

(b) In this activity what question did you ask yourself?

_____

(c) What predictions (hypothesis) did you make? _____

_____

_____

(d) How reliable and fair was your activity? _____

_____

_____

(e) What safety features did you consider and what did you do to reduce the risks?

_____

_____

(f) Identify controls in the activity. _____

_____

_____

(g) Identify any relevant dependent/independent/fixed variables in the activity.

_____

_____

(h) Record your results. _____

_____

_____

(i) What conclusion(s) did you reach? _____

_____

Reflection

(j) What are two things you liked about this activity?

- _____

- _____

(k) What did you find difficult about this activity? _____

_____

(l) If you were to do this activity again, what would you do differently?

_____

_____

Activity 28.2: Can we design a device to transform energy from one form to another?

(a) Date on which you carried out this activity _____

(b) In this activity what question did you ask yourself?

_____

(c) What predictions (hypothesis) did you make? _____

_____

_____

(d) How reliable and fair was your activity? _____

_____

_____

(e) What safety features did you consider and what did you do to reduce the risks?

_____

_____

(f) Identify controls in the activity. _____

_____

_____

(g) Identify any relevant dependent/independent/fixed variables in the activity.

_____

_____

(h) Record your observations. _____

_____

_____

(i) Draw and label a simple diagram of the equipment you used.

(j) What conclusion(s) did you reach? _____

_____

(k) **What are two things you liked about this activity?**

- _____

- _____

(l) **What did you find difficult about this activity?** _____

_____

(m) **If you were to do this activity again, what would you do differently?**

_____

Self evaluation – Energy

Now that you have completed this chapter, how well do you feel you understand each of the following (tick the relevant column)?

Topic	😊	😐	☹
Energy			
Energy conservation			
Energy dissipation			
Energy change			
Energy efficiency			

Action plan: **What I need to do to improve my learning** _____

_____

CHAPTER 29 HEAT

Log onto www.edcolearning.ie to find the Mind Map for this chapter.

Homework questions

1 Give three examples of where heat energy is changed to other forms.

(i) _____

(ii) _____

(iii) _____

2 Draw a line between the phrase on the left and the term that matches it on the right.

Feeling unwell	Thermometer
Scale for measuring temperature	°C
Used to measure temperature	Liquid in glass
Same temperature as −40°F	High body temperature
Absolute zero	−273.15°C
A type of thermometer	−40°C

3 We know that solids, liquids and gases expand when heated and contract when cooled. Using these ideas, briefly explain the following.

(a) When you buy a bottle of water in a shop it is never completely full.

_____

_____

(b) Small gaps are found in railway tracks. _____

_____

_____

(c) The mercury level can rise or fall in a thermometer.

_____

_____

(d) Electrical cables between pylons sag a little. _____

_____

_____

4 (a) Name the three ways by which heat energy can be transferred.

(i) _____

(ii) _____

(iii) _____

(b) Give one example of each of the three ways by which heat energy can be transferred.

(i) _____

(ii) _____

(iii) _____

5 **Keywords.** Write one short sentence using each of the following words:

(a) Heat _____

(b) Temperature _____

(c) Thermometer _____

(d) Expansion _____

(e) Contraction _____

(f) Latent heat _____

(g) Conduction _____

(h) Convection _____

(i) Radiation _____

Activity 29.1: What are the temperatures of everyday items?

(a) Date on which you carried out this activity _____

(b) In this activity what question did you ask yourself?

_____

(c) What predictions (hypothesis) did you make?

_____

(d) How reliable and fair was your activity?

_____

(e) What safety features did you consider and what did you do to reduce the risks?

_____

(f) Identify controls in the activity.

_____

(g) Identify any relevant dependent/independent/fixed variables in the activity.

_____

(h) **Record your results in the following table.**

Everyday items	Your measurement: Temperature (°C)	Classmate's measurement: Temperature (°C)
Air		
Warm tap water		
Cold tap water		
Cold water from a fridge		
Ice from a freezer		

(i) **Draw and label a simple diagram of the laboratory thermometer that you used.**

(j) **What conclusion(s) did you reach?** _____

_____

_____

Reflection

(k) **What are two things you liked about this activity?**

- _____

- _____

(l) **What did you find difficult about this activity?** _____

_____

(m) **If you were to do this activity again, what would you do differently?**

_____

_____

Activity 29.2: **How does heating and cooling of solids affect their expansion and contraction?**

(a) Date on which you carried out this activity _____

(b) In this activity what question did you ask yourself?

_____

(c) What predictions (hypothesis) did you make? _____

_____

_____

(d) How reliable and fair was your activity?

_____

(e) What safety features did you consider and what did you do to reduce the risks?

_____

(f) Identify controls in the activity.

_____

(g) Identify any relevant dependent/independent/fixed variables in the activity.

_____

(h) Record your observations. _____

_____

_____

(i) Draw and label a simple diagram of your equipment.

(j) What conclusion(s) did you reach? _____

_____

_____

Activity 29.3: How does heating and cooling of liquids affect their expansion and contraction?

(a) Date on which you carried out this activity _____

(b) In this activity what question did you ask yourself?

_____

(c) What predictions (hypothesis) did you make? _____

_____

_____

(d) How reliable and fair was your activity?

_____

(e) What safety features did you consider and what did you do to reduce the risks?

_____

(f) Identify controls in the activity.

_____

(g) Identify any relevant dependent/independent/fixed variables in the activity.

_____

(h) Record your observations. _____

_____

(i) Draw and label a diagram of your equipment.

(j) What conclusion(s) did you reach? _____

_____

Activity 29.4: How does heating and cooling of gases affect their expansion and contraction?

(a) Date on which you carried out this activity _____

(b) In this activity what question did you ask yourself?

_____

(c) What predictions (hypothesis) did you make? _____

_____

(d) How reliable and fair was your activity?

_____

(e) What safety features did you consider and what did you do to reduce the risks?

_____

(f) Identify controls in the activity.

_____

(g) Identify any relevant dependent/independent/fixed variables in the activity.

_____

(h) Record your observations. _____

_____

_____

(i) Draw and label a simple diagram of your equipment.

(j) What conclusion(s) did you reach?

_____

_____

Reflection

(k) What are two things you liked about activities 29.2, 29.3 and 29.4?

- _____

- _____

(l) What did you find difficult about these activities?

_____

_____

(m) If you were to do these activities again, what would you do differently?

_____

_____

Activity 29.5: How can we show that heating something may not change the temperature?

(a) Date on which you carried out this activity _____

(b) In this activity what question did you ask yourself?

_____

(c) What predictions (hypothesis) did you make? _____

_____

_____

(d) How reliable and fair was your activity? _____

_____

_____

(e) What safety features did you consider and what did you do to reduce the risks?

_____

_____

(f) Identify any controls in the activity.

_____

(g) Record your results. _____

_____

_____

(h) In the space below draw a simple diagram of the apparatus that you used for this activity.

(i) What conclusion(s) did you reach? _____

_____

_____

Reflection

(j)   What are two things you liked about this activity?

  •   _____

  •   _____

(k)   What did you find difficult about this activity? _____

_____

(l)   If you were to do this activity again, what would you do differently?

_____

_____

Self evaluation – Heat

Now that you have completed this chapter, how well do you feel you understand each of the following (tick the relevant column)?

Topic	😊	😐	🙁
Heat			
Temperature			
Thermometer			
Expansion			
Contraction			
Latent heat			
Conduction			
Convection			
Radiation			

Action plan: What I need to do to improve my learning _____

_____

ELECTRICITY – CURRENT ELECTRICITY

Log onto www.edcolearning.ie to find the **Mind Map** for this chapter.

Homework questions

1 Draw a line between the explanation on the left and the term it is describing on the right.

The unit of current	Ohm
The unit of voltage (potential difference)	Ampere
The unit of resistance	Voltmeter
The instrument to measure current	Ohmmeter
The instrument to measure voltage (potential difference)	Volt
The instrument to measure resistance	Ammeter

2 Complete the table below by drawing in the symbol of the item of equipment.

Name of equipment	Symbol
Filament lamp	
Resistor	
Ammeter	
Battery	
Switch	
Variable resistor	
Voltmeter	

3 Using the formula triangle below, complete the following table, (a)–(i).

$$\frac{V}{I \times R}$$

Voltage	Current (ampere)	Resistance (ohm)
12	2	(a)
12	(b)	10
(c)	5	46
6	0.5	(d)
6	(e)	200
(f)	0.02	1000
230	10	(g)
230	(h)	100
(i)	0.5	10 000

4 (a) Draw a circuit diagram to show three bulbs connected in series and with a 3 V battery in the circuit.

(b) Draw a circuit diagram to show three bulbs connected in parallel and with a 3 V battery in the circuit.

5 **Keywords.** Write one short sentence using each of the following words:

(a) Current _____

(b) Potential difference _____

(c) Voltage _____

(d) Resistance _____

(e) Ammeter _____

(f) Voltmeter _____

(g) Ohmmeter _____

(h) Electrons _____

(i) Conventional current _____

(j) Battery _____

(k) Switch _____

(l) Lamp _____

(m) Filament bulb _____

Activity 30.1: How can we demonstrate an electrical circuit?

(a) Date on which you carried out this activity _____

(b) In this activity what question did you ask yourself?

_____

(c) What predictions (hypothesis) did you make?

_____

(d) How reliable and fair was your activity?

_____

(e) What safety features did you consider and what did you do to reduce the risks?

_____

(f) Identify controls in the activity.

_____

(g) Identify any relevant dependent/independent/fixed variables in the activity.

_____

(h) Record your observations.

_____

(i) Draw and label a simple diagram of the class circuit (there is no need to draw in every lead).

(j) What conclusion(s) did you reach?

_____

_____

Reflection

(k) What are two things you liked about this activity?

- _____

- _____

(l)   What did you find difficult about this activity?

_____

_____

(m)   If you were to do this activity again, what would you do differently?

_____

_____

Activity 30.2: How do we measure current?

(a)   Date on which you carried out this activity _____

(b)   In this activity what question did you ask yourself?

_____

(c)   What predictions (hypothesis) did you make?

_____

_____

(d)   How reliable and fair was your activity?

_____

(e)   What safety features did you consider and what did you do to reduce the risks?

_____

(f)   Identify any controls in the activity.

_____

(g)   Record your observations.

_____

_____

(h)   In the space below draw a simple diagram of the apparatus that you used for this activity.

(i)   What conclusion(s) did you reach?

_____

_____

Activity 30.3: **How do we measure voltage?**

(a) Date on which you carried out this activity _____

(b) In this activity what question did you ask yourself?

_____

(c) What predictions (hypothesis) did you make?

_____

_____

(d) How reliable and fair was your activity?

_____

(e) What safety features did you consider and what did you do to reduce the risks?

_____

(f) Identify any controls in the activity.

_____

(g) Record your observations.

_____

_____

(h) In the space below draw a simple diagram of the apparatus that you used for this activity.

(i) What conclusion(s) did you reach?

_____

_____

Reflection

(j) What are two things you liked activity 30.2 and activity 30.3?

• _____

• _____

(k) What did you find difficult about activity 30.2 and activity 30.3?

_____

_____

(l) If you were to do activity 30.2 and activity 30.3 again, what would you do differently?

_____

_____

Activity 30.4: How can we see the relationship between current and voltage?

(a) Date on which you carried out this activity _____

(b) In this activity what question did you ask yourself?

_____

(c) What predictions (hypothesis) did you make?

_____

_____

(d) How reliable and fair was your activity?

_____

(e) What safety features did you consider and what did you do to reduce the risks?

_____

(f) Identify controls in the activity.

_____

(g) Identify any relevant variables in the activity.

_____

(h) Record your results in the following table.

Voltage (V)	Current (A)

(i)   Create a graph of your results (Voltage on the *y*-axis and Current on the *x*-axis).

(j)   Draw and label a diagram of your circuit.

(k)   How do you change the size of the current flowing in the circuit?

_____

(l)   What exactly does a switch do to stop the current from flowing?

_____

(m)   What do you do to make sure the temperature of the resistor stays constant?

_____

Reflection

(n)   What are two things you liked about this activity?

•   _____

•   _____

(o)   What did you find difficult about this activity?

_____

(p)   If you were to do this activity again, what would you do differently?

_____

Self evaluation – Electricity – current electricity

Now that you have completed this chapter, how well do you feel you understand each of the following (tick the relevant column)?

Topic	🙂	😐	🙁
Current			
Potential difference			
Voltage			
Resistance			
Measuring current with an ammeter			
Measuring voltage with a voltmeter			
Doing calculations using: $\dfrac{V}{I \times R}$			

Action plan: **What I need to do to improve my learning** _____

_____

ISSUES THAT ARISE FROM GENERATION AND USE OF ELECTRICITY

Log onto **www.edcolearning.ie** to find the **Mind Map** for this chapter.

Homework questions

1. Calculate the power used by an electrical appliance that consumes 6 amperes of current when connected to a 230 volt supply. _____

_____

2. Calculate the power used by an electrical appliance that consumes 2 amperes of current when connected to a 110 volt supply. _____

_____

3. Calculate the power used by an electrical appliance that consumes 0.2 amperes of current when connected to a 12 volt supply. _____

_____

4. Calculate the current used by an electric kettle rated 1150 watts when it is plugged into the socket at home, which gives 230 volts. _____

_____

5. Calculate the current used by a flat-screen TV rated 115 watts when it is plugged into the socket at home, which gives 230 volts. _____

_____

6. Calculate the current used by a portable vacuum cleaner rated 24 watts when it is plugged into the socket in a car, which gives 12 volts. _____

_____

7. Calculate the potential difference (voltage) applied when a 30 watt car bulb uses a current of 2.5 amperes. _____

_____

8. Calculate the potential difference (voltage) applied when an 11 watt bulb uses a current of 0.05 amperes. _____

_____

9 Calculate the potential difference (voltage) applied when a 660 watt appliance uses a current of 6 amperes. _____

_____

10 An electric kettle has a power rating of 2.8 kW. The kettle is used to boil water for a total of 1 hour each day for a full week.

   (a) Calculate the number of units of electricity used in the week.

_____

   (b) Calculate the total cost if 1 kWh costs 18 cents.

_____

11 An electric shower has a power rating of 5 kW. The shower is used for a total of 1 hour each day for 4 full weeks.

   (a) Calculate the number of units of electricity used in the 4 weeks.

_____

_____

   (b) Calculate the total cost if 1 kWh costs 18 cents.

_____

_____

12 An electrical appliance has a power rating of 800 W. The appliance is used for a total of 1.5 hours each day for 8 full weeks.

   (a) Calculate the number of units of electricity used in the 8 weeks.

_____

_____

   (b) Calculate the total cost if 1 kWh costs 18 cents.

_____

_____

13 **Keywords.** Write one short sentence using each of the following words:

   (a) Fossil fuels _____

   (b) Nuclear fuels _____

   (c) Geothermal energy _____

   (d) Solar cells _____

   (e) Electrical power _____

   (f) Watt _____

   (g) Kilowatt-hour _____

(h) Sustainable _____

(i) Wire coil _____

(j) Magnet _____

(k) Turbine generator _____

Activity 31.1: How can we generate electricity?

(a) Date on which you carried out this activity _____

(b) In this activity what question did you ask yourself?

_____

(c) What predictions (hypothesis) did you make?

_____

_____

(d) How reliable and fair was your activity?

_____

(e) What safety features did you consider and what did you do to reduce the risks?

_____

(f) Identify controls in the activity.

_____

(g) Identify any relevant dependent/independent/fixed variables in the activity.

_____

(h) Record your observations.

_____

_____

_____

_____

(i) Draw and label a diagram of the equipment you used.

(j) What conclusion(s) did you reach?

_____

_____

_____

Activity 31.2: How can we generate electricity from solar cells?

(a) Date on which you carried out this activity _____

(b) In this activity what question did you ask yourself?

_____

(c) What predictions (hypothesis) did you make? _____

_____

(d) How reliable and fair was your activity?

_____

(e) What safety features did you consider and what did you do to reduce the risks?

_____

(f) Identify controls in the activity.

_____

(g) Identify any relevant dependent/independent/fixed variables in the activity.

_____

(h) Record your readings from the multimeter. _____

_____

_____

_____

(i) Draw and label a simple diagram of the equipment you used.

(j) What conclusion(s) did you reach? _____

_____

_____

(k) What did you observe when you moved the lamp nearer the solar cells?

- _____

- _____

(l) What did you observe when you covered some of the solar cells with a piece of paper (that is, reduced the area of the solar cells that is exposed to the light)?

- _____

- _____

Activity 31.3: How can we estimate the cost of electricity in our homes for a week?

(a) Dates on which you carried out this activity _____

(b) In this activity what question did you ask yourself?

_____

(c) What predictions (hypothesis) did you make? _____

_____

(d) How reliable and fair was your activity?

_____

(e) What safety features did you consider and what did you do to reduce the risks?

_____

(f) Record your results in the table below.

Appliance	Power rating (kW)	Estimate of number of hours of usage in 1 week	Estimate of number of kilowatt-hours

Total number of kilowatt-hours: _____

Cost per unit: _____

Estimated cost of electricity for 1 week: _____

_____

(g) What conclusion(s) did you reach? _____

_____

Reflection

(h) What are two things you liked about activities 31.1, 31.2 and 31.3?

- _____

- _____

(i) What did you find difficult about activities 31.1, 31.2 and 31.3?

_____

_____

_____

(j) If you were to do these activities again, what would you do differently?

_____

_____

_____

_____

Self evaluation – Issues that arise from generation and use of electricity

Now that you have completed this chapter, how well do you feel you understand each of the following (tick the relevant column)?

Topic	🙂	😐	🙁
Ways of generating electricity			
Energy from fossil fuels			
Energy from nuclear fuels			
Energy from the wind			
Energy from moving water			
Geothermal energy			
Energy from solar cells			
Electrical power			
The unit of electrical energy			
The power rating of electrical appliances			
Reducing consumption of electrical energy			

Action plan: What I need to do to improve my learning _____

_____

CHAPTER 32

ELECTRONICS

📄 Log onto **www.edcolearning.ie** to find the **Mind Map** for this chapter.

Homework questions

1 Complete the table below by drawing in the matching symbol.

Name	Symbol
Buzzer	
Diode	
Light-emitting diode (LED)	
Light-dependent resistor (LDR)	

2 Draw a circuit diagram showing a diode connected to a battery in forward bias.

3 Draw a circuit diagram showing a diode connected to a battery in reverse bias.

4 How do you change the resistance of an LDR from a very high resistance to a very low resistance? _____

_____

5 Draw a circuit diagram showing an LED connected to a battery so that it is emitting light.

6 Draw a circuit diagram showing an LED connected to a battery so that it does not emit light.

7 **Keywords.** Write one short sentence using each of the following words:

(a) Buzzer _____

(b) Diode _____

(c) Forward bias _____

(d) Reverse bias _____

(e) Light-emitting diode (LED) _____

(f) Light-dependent resistor (LDR) _____

Activity 32.1: What happens when a diode and a bulb are connected to a battery?

(a) Date on which you carried out this activity _____

(b) In this activity what question did you ask yourself?

_____

(c) What predictions (hypothesis) did you make? _____

_____

(d) How reliable and fair was your activity? _____

_____

(e) What safety features did you consider and what did you do to reduce the risks?

_____

(f) Record your observations. _____

_____

_____

(g) Draw and label diagrams of the circuits.

Diode connected first way   Diode connected second way

(h) What conclusion(s) did you reach? _____

_____

_____

Activity 32.2: When does an LED emit light?

(a) Date on which you carried out this activity

_____

(b) In this activity what question did you ask yourself?

_____

(c) What predictions (hypothesis) did you make? _____

_____

(d) How reliable and fair was your activity?

_____

(e) What safety features did you consider and what did you do to reduce the risks?

_____

(f) In the space below draw the diagrams of the apparatus that you used.

Part (a)   Part (b)

(g) Under what condition will the LED emit light?

_____

(h) Under what condition will the LED not emit light?

_____

(i) What are the terms used for when an LED will emit light and when it will not emit light?

_____

Activity 32.3: What factor controls the resistance of an LDR and the current flowing through it?

(a) Date on which you carried out this activity _____

(b) In this activity what question did you ask yourself?

_____

(c) What predictions (hypothesis) did you make? _____

_____

(d) How reliable and fair was your activity?

_____

(e) What safety features did you consider and what did you do to reduce the risks?

_____

(f) Record your observations and values of resistance.

(g) In the space below draw the diagrams of the apparatus that you used for this activity.

Part (a)   Part (b)

Activity 32.4: How can we set up a circuit to choose between a high-frequency buzzer and a low-frequency buzzer?

(a) Date on which you carried out this activity _____

(b) In this activity what question did you ask yourself?

_____

(c) What predictions (hypothesis) did you make? _____

_____

(d) How reliable and fair was your activity? _____

_____

(e) What safety features did you consider and what did you do to reduce the risks?

_____

(f) Record your observations and explanations. _____

_____

_____

_____

(g) Draw and label a diagram of your circuit.

(h) What conclusion(s) did you reach? _____

_____

_____

(i) How did you activate the high-frequency buzzer? _____

_____

(j) How did you activate the low-frequency buzzer? _____

_____

(k) What would you do to activate the two buzzers at the same time?

_____

_____

Activity 32.5: How can we choose which LED will emit light?

(a) Date on which you carried out this activity _____

(b) In this activity what question did you ask yourself?

_____

(c) What predictions (hypothesis) did you make? _____

_____

(d) How reliable and fair was your activity? _____

_____

(e) What safety features did you consider and what did you do to reduce the risks?

_____

_____

(f) Record your observations and explanations.

Closing switch A _____

_____

Closing switch B _____

_____

Closing switches A and B _____

_____

(g) Draw and label a diagram of your circuit.

(h) What conclusion(s) did you reach? _____

_____

_____

✎ **Activity 32.6:** **How can we activate a buzzer by switching on a light?**

(a) Date on which you carried out this activity _____

(b) In this activity what question did you ask yourself? _____

_____

_____

(c) What predictions (hypothesis) did you make? _____

_____

_____

(d) How reliable and fair was your activity? _____

_____

(e) What safety features did you consider and what did you do to reduce the risks?

_____

_____

(f) Identify controls in the activity. _____

_____

(g) Identify any relevant dependent/independent/fixed variables in the activity.

_____

_____

(h) Record your observations. _____

_____

_____

_____

(i) Draw and label a diagram of your circuit.

(j) What conclusion(s) did you reach? _____

_____

_____

Reflection

(k) **What are two things you liked about the activities in this section?**

- _____

- _____

(l) **What did you find difficult about the activities in this section?**

_____

_____

(m) **If you were to do these activities again, what would you do differently?**

_____

_____

Self evaluation – Electronics

Now that you have completed this chapter, how well do you feel you understand each of the following (tick the relevant column)?

Topic	🙂	😐	🙁
Symbol for a buzzer			
Symbol for a diode			
Symbol for an LED			
Symbol for an LDR			
Why an LED needs a resistor			
Forward bias			
Reverse bias			

Action plan: **What I need to do to improve my learning** _____

_____

CHAPTER 33 — IMPACT OF MODERN PHYSICS ON SOCIETY

Log onto **www.edcolearning.ie** to find the **Mind Map** for this chapter.

Homework questions

1   In the space provided below give two brief accounts of how telecommunications have affected each of science, society and the environment.

   (a) How telecommunications have affected science:

      (i) _____

      (ii) _____

   (b) How telecommunications have affected society:

      (i) _____

      (ii) _____

   (c) How telecommunications have affected the environment:

      (i) _____

      (ii) _____

2   In the space provided below give two brief accounts of how the internet has affected each of science, society and the environment.

   (a) How the internet has affected science:

      (i) _____
      _____

      (ii) _____
      _____

   (b) How the internet has affected society:

      (i) _____
      _____

      (ii) _____
      _____

   (c) How the internet has affected the environment:

      (i) _____
      _____

      (ii) _____
      _____

3 Using the figures in the table, plot the information given on the graph with the number of millions on the *y*-axis and the years on the *x*-axis.

At the end of the year	Number of people using the internet
1995	16 million
1999	248 million
2003	719 million
2006	1093 million
2009	1802 million
2012	2497 million

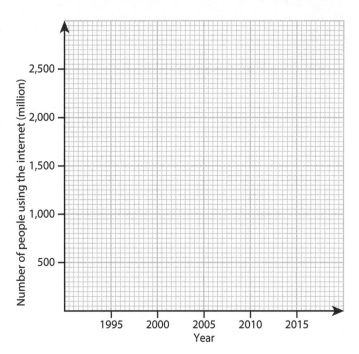

4 **Keywords.** Write one short sentence using each of the following words:

(a) Digital electronics _____

(b) Telecommunications _____

(c) Internet _____

Self evaluation – Impact of modern physics on society

Now that you have completed this chapter, how well do you feel you understand each of the following (tick the relevant column)?

Topic	🙂	😐	🙁
Digital electronics			
Digital signals			
Telecommunications			
The impact of telecommunications on society, science and the environment			
The internet			
The impacts of the internet on society, science and the environment			
How the numbers of users on the internet is growing			
Reliability of information from the internet			

Action plan: What I need to do to improve my learning _____

_____

Peer Assessment

Date:__/__/__

Your name	Name of lab partner	Title of work

Success Criteria	How did this piece of work achieve the success criteria?

Two excellent points	This could be improved by…
1	
2	

CHAPTER 34

THE BIG BANG – HOW OUR UNIVERSE BEGAN

Log onto **www.edcolearning.ie** to find the **Mind Map** for this chapter.

Homework questions

1 Outline the major fact that Edwin Hubble noted about our universe.

IN 1929, US astronomer Hubble Galaxies are moving away from each other. The farther away a galaxy is, the faster the galaxy is moving away from us.

2 How old is our universe?

13.8 BILLION YRS OLD

3 In what year was the Hubble Space Telescope launched?

1990 BY NASA

4 Name the space agency that launched the Hubble Space Telescope.

NASA IN USA

5 Explain the term 'singularity'.

is a zone that is very very small, very very dense and very very hot.

6 Identify a term that best describes the way in which the universe is getting bigger.

Expanding

7 Name the force that was present within the singularity.

Gravity

8 Outline how matter was formed following the Big Bang.

the matter produced in the Big bang gathered into stars & galaxies

9 Explain the term 'force of gravity'.

Force of Gravity or the gravitational pull is what pulls objects together

10 Outline, in the correct sequence, the events that took place during the Big Bang. Use the following words in your account:

singularity ~~expand~~ light ~~matter~~ ~~temperature~~ ~~dense~~ particles

In the first moments after the Big Bang, the singularity was extremely dense & the tempreture was very hot. As the Universe began to expand & cool things happened more slowly. And after 250,000 to 300,000 year our the Universe went from Opaque to transparent at this point. Astron-omical & physical calculations suggests that the visible universe is only 4% of what the universe is actually made of. 26% is made of an unknown type of matter called 'Dark matter'.

11 Keywords. Write one short sentence using each of the following words:

(a) **Solar system** the collection of 8 planets & their moons in or Around the sun.

(b) **Singularity** A zone that is very dense, hot & small

(c) **Expanding universe** it has been growing ever since the big ba

(d) **Galaxies** A galaxy is made up of gas, dust & stars

(e) **Astronomer** Someone who studies space

(f) **Gravity** a invisible force that pulls objects towards each other.

Activity 34.2: How can we visualise how the universe is expanding?

(a) Date on which you carried out this activity _____

(b) In this activity what question did you ask yourself?

What materials would be in the gravity how big would it be?

(c) What predictions (hypothesis) did you make?

_____

_____

(d) How reliable and fair was your activity?

_____

_____

(e) What safety features did you consider and what did you do to reduce the risks?

_____

_____

(f) Identify controls in the activity.

_____

_____

(g) Identify any relevant dependent/independent/fixed variables in the activity.

_____

_____

(h) Record your results in the table below.

Dot number	Distance from next dot when balloon has little air in it	Distance from next dot when balloon is blown up

(i)   What conclusion(s) did you reach?

_____

_____

_____

Reflection

(j)   What are two things you liked about this activity?

• ___Homework   questions_____

• _____

(k)   What did you find difficult about this activity?

___The   definitions_____

_____

(l)   If you were to do this activity again, what would you do differently?

_____

_____

Self evaluation – The Big Bang – how our universe began

Now that you have completed this chapter, how well do you feel you understand each of the following (tick the relevant column)?

Topic	🙂	😐	☹️
The meaning of the word 'astronomy'	✓		
The Hubble Space Telescope	✓		
Hubble's main conclusion	✓		
The age of the universe	✓		
Singularity	✓		
How the 'Big Bang' took place	✓		
What force allowed galaxies to form		✓	✓
Galaxies	✓		

Action plan: What I need to do to improve my learning _____

_____

_____

GALAXIES, STARS AND THE SOLAR SYSTEM

Log onto **www.edcolearning.ie** to find the **Mind Map** for this chapter.

Homework questions

1 Explain the term 'star'. A star is a luminous object which can produce its own light & heat

2 Identify the element that is used up in the nuclear reactions within a star.

Hydrogen

3 Name the two products that are released from a nuclear reaction.

(i) heat

(ii) light

4 Describe the term 'nebulae'. Large gas clouds in space. The

5 Name the four stages in the life cycle of a star.

(i) Formation

(ii) Stable Period

(iii) Red giant

(iv) White dwarf

6 Identify the key points of each of the four stages in the life cycle of a star.

(i) Gas particles collapse on each other causing nuclear fusion to take place & Star is born

(ii) Star becomes stable.

(iii) Burns off helium.

(iv) Burns light

7 In which phase of the life cycle is our Sun?

Stable Period

8 Outline why a star turns into a red giant. When a star has used up its supply of hydrogen it begins to burn helium on its outer parts.

9 Explain the term 'galaxy'. A galaxy is a collection of millions of stars, dust, comets, asteriods and all celestial bodies.

10 What is the name of our galaxy?

Milky Way

11 Explain the term 'solar system'. The solar system is made up of the Sun and the planets that orbit around it

12 Describe the term 'planet'. To be a planet there are 3 rules. 1: You must orbit the Sun 2: You must be strong enough to pull yourself into a spherical shape. 3. You must be able to clear your orbit.

13 List the three types of planet found within the solar system and give a named example of a planet for each type of planet.

(i) Planetoid/Dwarf planet - Pluto

(ii) Jovian - Jupiter

(iii) Terrestrial - Venus.

14 Explain why planets orbit around the Sun. Planets orbit the Sun bcz the Sun tries to 'pull' the planets towards them at the same time the planets are trying to pull away. This results in a rotation

15 Draw a diagram showing the arrangement of the planets and the Sun in the solar system.

16 Gravity is a force that 'pulls' objects that have a mass towards the Earth. A hammer and a feather have two very different masses; a hammer has a much greater mass than a feather.

Using your knowledge of gravity (or more correctly in science terms, acceleration due to gravity), on Earth and on other bodies in the solar system, explain whether the hammer or the feather will hit the ground first on the following:

(i) Earth

(ii) The Moon

17 Keywords. Write one short sentence using each of the following words:

(a) Star _A luminous object which gives off light & heat._

(b) Nuclear fusion _When 2 hydrogen atoms fused together_

(c) Red giant _3rd stage of a star_

(d) Nebula _Large gas clouds in space._

(e) White dwarf _4th stage of a star_

(f) Luminous _Give off light + heat._

(g) Supernova _Where an star explodes._

(h) Planetoid _Dwarf planet_

(i) Jovian _Planet made out of gas_

(j) Planet _Orbits the Sun. etc_

(k) Main sequence _Star becomes this in the Stable Period_

(l) Solar system _Made up of the Sun and planets._

(m) Terrestrial _Made up of rock and metal._

Self evaluation – Galaxies, stars and the solar system

Now that you have completed this chapter, how well do you feel you understand each of the following (tick the relevant column)?

Topic	🙂	😐	🙁
The meaning of the term 'luminous'	✓		
The type of reactions that take place in a star	✓		
The four phases of the life cycle	✓		
Galaxies	✓		
The name of our galaxy	✓		
The shape of our galaxy	✓		
Our solar system	✓		
The three types of planets in the solar system	✓		✓
The difference between Earth and other planets in the solar system		✓	

Action plan: What I need to do to improve my learning _____

_____

_____

Log onto **www.edcolearning.ie** to find the **Mind Map** for this chapter.

Homework questions

1   Identify the age of the solar system.

_____

2   Name two places in the solar system where comets are located.

(i)   _____

(ii) _____

3   Explain the key difference between the two areas containing the comets (as identified in question 2).

_____

_____

4   Describe the composition of comets.

_____

_____

_____

5   Outline how the tails on a comet are formed.

_____

_____

6   In which direction do comets' tails stretch?

_____

7   List two features that asteroids lack in comparison to Earth.

(i)   _____

(ii) _____

8   Identify a term that best describes a small asteroid.

_____

9 Identify a term that best describes a large asteroid.

_____

10 Name two asteroids that are currently being studied by NASA.

(i) _____

(ii) _____

11 Write the letter of the definition on the right that matches the word on the left.

(i)   Nuclear fusion _____   (a) Name of our galaxy

(ii) Milky Way _____   (b) Mysterious energy within the universe

(iii) Gravity _____   (c) The last stage of a star's life

(iv) Hubble _____   (d) The Sun in this form will destroy Earth

(v)   Terrestrial _____   (e) Reactions that take place in the Sun

(vi) Planetoid _____   (f) The type of planet that Earth is an example of

(vii) Red giant _____   (g) Name of a famous telescope

(viii) White dwarf _____   (h) Pluto is an example of this

12 Using the table below, compare comets and asteroids by explaining the differences in four different features.

Comets	Asteroids

13 Keywords. Write one short sentence using each of the following words:

(a) Comets _____

_____

_____

(b) Asteroids _____

_____

_____

(c) Meteors _____

_____

_____

(d) Meteorites _____

_____

_____

(e) Meteoroids _____

_____

_____

Self evaluation – Comets, asteroids and meteors

Now that you have completed this chapter, how well do you feel you understand each of the following (tick the relevant column)?

Topic	🙂	😐	🙁
The age of comets			
What comets are			
Where comets are located in the solar system			
What forms the tails of comets			
Where asteroids are located in the solar system			
The three types of asteroid			
Meteors			
Meteorites			
Meteoroids			
The damage asteroids can cause to Earth			
The advantages Earth has received from comets			

Action plan: What I need to do to improve my learning _____

_____

_____

TO THE MOON AND BEYOND

Log onto **www.edcolearning.ie** to find the **Mind Map** for this chapter.

Homework questions

1 Outline how the Moon has made Earth stable.

_____

2 How do scientists define the term 'moon'?

_____

_____

3 Describe how our moon was formed.

_____

_____

4 How old is the Moon?

_____

5 How long does it take for the Moon to revolve once around Earth?

_____

6 Outline the distance between the Moon and Earth.

_____

7 The Moon does not produce its own light. Identify the term that describes this.

_____

8 Name three moons that are located in the solar system.

(i) _____

(ii) _____

(iii) _____

9 Name the planets that the moons you named in question 8 revolve around.

(i) _____

(ii) _____

(iii) _____

10 Explain the two forms of tides shown in the diagram. Use the positions of the Sun and Moon, relative to Earth, in your explanation.

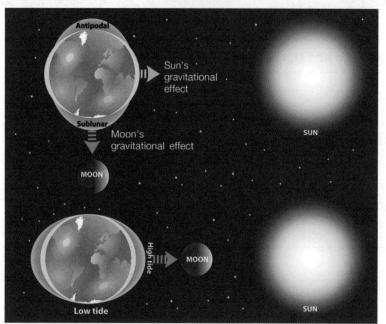

_____

_____

_____

_____

_____

_____

_____

11 Compare each of the moons you named in question 8, in terms of gravity, and their atmospheres.

(i) _____

(ii) _____

(iii) _____

12 The diagram shows the rotation and revolution of the Moon around Earth and Earth around the Sun. Match the correct number of days with the terms in the table below and add an explanation of each term.

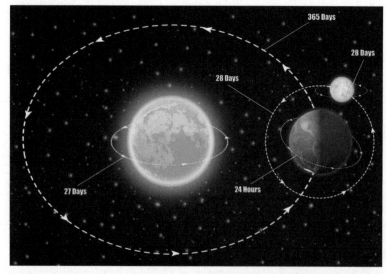

Terms:
Rotate
Orbit
Revolves

Number of days	Term	Explanation
1		
365		
28		

13 **Keywords.** Write one short sentence using each of the following words:

(a) Revolve _____

(b) Satellite _____

(c) Atmosphere _____

(d) Gravitational _____

(e) Rotation _____

(f) Reflect _____

(g) Tides _____

(h) Moon _____

(i) Non-luminous _____

Activity 37.1: How can we demonstrate that we see only one side of the Moon?

(a) Date on which you carried out this activity _____

(b) In this activity what question did you ask yourself?

_____

(c) What predictions (hypothesis) did you make?

_____

_____

(d) How reliable and fair was your activity?

_____

_____

(e) What safety features did you consider and what did you do to reduce the risks?

_____

_____

(f) Identify controls in the activity. _____

_____

(g) Identify any relevant dependent/independent/fixed variables in the activity.

_____

_____

(h) What happened to the smaller ball as you moved it around the larger one?

_____

_____

(i) **What conclusions did you reach?**

_____

_____

Reflection

(j) **What are two things you liked about this activity?**

• _____

• _____

(k) **What did you find difficult about this activity?**

_____

(l) **If you were to do this activity again, what would you do differently?**

_____

_____

Self evaluation – To the Moon and beyond

Now that you have completed this chapter, how well do you feel you understand each of the following (tick the relevant column)?

Topic	🙂	😐	🙁
What a moon is			
How far away the Moon is from Earth			
How the Moon was formed			
How long it takes the Moon to revolve around Earth			
What the terms 'revolve' and 'rotate' mean			
The three types of asteroid			
Why we see only one side of the Moon from Earth			
The age of the Moon			
What the force of gravity on the Moon is in comparison to Earth			
The names of other moons in the solar system			
The names of the planets that those moons revolve around			
How Earth compares to moons in the solar system			

Action plan: **What I need to do to improve my learning** _____

_____

_____

CHAPTER 38
EARTH, SUN AND MOON – IT'S ALL RELATIVE

Log onto **www.edcolearning.ie** to find the **Mind Map** for this chapter.

Homework questions

1   Distinguish clearly between Earth, the Sun and the Moon. _____
_____

2   Explain what the 'phases' of the Moon are based on. _____
_____
_____

3   Describe a 'crescent' Moon. _____
_____

4   Explain the term 'gibbous'. _____
_____

5   How many phases of the Moon are there? _____

6   List the phases of the Moon in order of appearance.

     Phase 1 _____

     Phase 2 _____

     Phase 3 _____

     Phase 4 _____

     Phase 5 _____

     Phase 6 _____

     Phase 7 _____

     Phase 8 _____

7   Identify the time in the year when the Earth is:

     (a)   Closest to the Sun _____

     (b)   Farthest from the Sun _____

8   Explain the axial tilt of Earth. _____
_____

9   Outline why we experience different seasons on Earth.

_____

_____

_____

_____

10   Explain how the tilt of rotation of Earth affects the length of the day.

_____

_____

_____

_____

11   Outline the positions of Earth, the Sun and the Moon during:

(a) A lunar eclipse _____

(b) A solar eclipse _____

12   Name the type of shadow that places Earth in total darkness.

_____

13 **Keywords.** Write one short sentence using each of the following words:

(a) Lunar _____

(b) Crescent _____

(c) Gibbous _____

(d) Axis _____

(e) Waxing _____

(f) Waning _____

(g) Seasons _____

(h) Eclipse _____

(i) Umbra _____

(j) Penumbra _____

(k) Totality _____

Activity 38.1: How can we develop and use a model of the Earth-Sun-Moon system?

(a) Date on which you carried out this activity _____

(b) In this activity what question did you ask yourself?

_____

(c) What predictions (hypothesis) did you make?

_____

_____

(d) How reliable and fair was your activity?

_____

_____

(e) What safety features did you consider and what did you do to reduce the risks?

_____

_____

(f) What did you learn about the phases of the Moon from your observations?

_____

_____

Reflection

(g) What are two things you liked about this activity?

• _____

• _____

(h) What did you find difficult about this activity? _____

_____

(i) If you were to do this activity again, what would you do differently?

_____

_____

✎ **Activity 38.2:** **How can we create our own lunar guides for a month?**

(a) **Lunar month:**

Week	Monday	Tuesday	Wednesday	Thursday	Friday	Saturday	Sunday
1							
2							
3							
4							
5							

(b) Were you able to see the Moon every night, or did you have to check the phases of the Moon some other way? Make notes on how you conducted this activity.

_____

_____

_____

(c) Do you think your observations were reliable? Say why they were or they were not.

_____

_____

(d) What did you learn about the phases of the Moon from your observations?

_____

_____

_____

Reflection

(e) What are two things you liked about this activity?

• _____

• _____

(f) What did you find difficult about this activity?

_____

_____

(g) If you were to do this activity again, what would you do differently?

_____

_____

Activity 38.3: How can we investigate Earth's tilt?

(a) Date on which you carried out this activity _____

(b) In this activity what question did you ask yourself?

_____

(c) What predictions (hypothesis) did you make?

_____

_____

(d) How reliable and fair was your activity?

_____

_____

(e) What safety features did you consider and what did you do to reduce the risks?

_____

_____

(f) Identify controls in the activity.

_____

_____

(g) Identify any relevant dependent/independent/fixed variables in the activity.

_____

_____

(h) Record your results.

Angle	Temperature (°C)	Number of squares the light covers

(i) What conclusion(s) did you reach?

_____

_____

_____

Reflection

(j) What are two things you liked about this activity?

- _____

- _____

(k) What did you find difficult about this activity? _____

_____

(l) If you were to do this activity again, what would you do differently?

_____

_____

Activity 38.4: How does a lunar eclipse occur?

(a) Date on which you carried out this activity _____

(b) In this activity what question did you ask yourself?

_____

(c) What predictions (hypothesis) did you make? _____

_____

(d) How reliable and fair was your activity? _____

_____

(e) What safety features did you consider and what did you do to reduce the risks?

_____

_____

(f) Identify controls in the activity. _____

_____

(g) Identify any relevant dependent/independent/fixed variables in the activity.

_____

_____

(h) Record your results:

   (i) For a lunar eclipse _____

   (ii) For a solar eclipse_____

(i)   What conclusion(s) did you reach? _____

_____

Reflection

(j)   What are two things you liked about this activity?

•   _____

•   _____

(k)   What did you find difficult about this activity? _____

_____

(l)   If you were to do this activity again, what would you do differently?

_____

_____

Self evaluation – Earth, Sun and Moon – it's all relative

Now that you have completed this chapter, how well do you feel you understand each of the following (tick the relevant column)?

Topic	🙂	😐	☹️
The phases of the Moon			
The meanings of 'waning', 'waxing' and 'gibbous'			
The cause of the seasons on Earth			
How Earth is affected by its tilted rotation			
The axis of Earth			
Lunar eclipse			
Solar eclipse			
The positions of Earth, the Sun and the Moon for both eclipses			
The umbra of an eclipse			
The penumbra of an eclipse			
Totality			

Action plan: What I need to do to improve my learning _____

_____

_____

Log onto **www.edcolearning.ie** to find the **Mind Map** for this chapter.

Homework questions

1 In what form(s) can water be found on Earth?

_____

_____

2 Outline why the water cycle is necessary for Earth and its inhabitants.

_____

_____

3 Name the six stages of the water cycle.

Stage 1 _____

Stage 2 _____

Stage 3 _____

Stage 4 _____

Stage 5 _____

Stage 6 _____

4 Using the names of the stages identified in question 3, fill in the labels on the diagram of the water cycle below.

5 Explain why water condenses as it rises up into the atmosphere.

_____

_____

_____

6 Explain the term 'infiltration'.

_____

_____

7 In what form is carbon found in the atmosphere?

_____

8 Using your own words, outline how fossil fuels are formed.

_____

_____

_____

9 Identify the force that pulls the water droplets of rain to the ground.

_____

10 Name the fossil fuels found on Earth.

_____

_____

11 List three forms of carbon in everyday life.

(i) _____

(ii) _____

(iii) _____

12 Name the stages of the carbon cycle in the correct order.

Stage 1 _____

Stage 2 _____

Stage 3 _____

Stage 4 _____

Stage 5 _____

Stage 6 _____

13 Explain the following terms and give an example of each:

Carbon sink _____

_____

Carbon source _____

_____

14 Keywords. Write one short sentence using each of the following words

(a) Evaporation _____

(b) Condensation _____

(c) Precipitation _____

(d) Organic _____

(e) Cycling _____

(f) Photosynthesis _____

(g) Carbon sink _____

(h) Respiration _____

(i) Carbon source _____

(j) Transpiration _____

(k) Decompose _____

Activity 39.1: How can we demonstrate evaporation?

(a) Date on which you carried out this activity _____

(b) In this activity what question did you ask yourself?

_____

(c) What predictions (hypothesis) did you make?

_____

(d) How reliable and fair was your activity?

_____

(e) What safety features did you consider and what did you do to reduce the risks?

_____

(f) Identify controls in the activity.

_____

(g) Identify any relevant dependent/independent/fixed variables in the activity.

_____

(h) Record your observations.

_____

_____

(i) What conclusion(s) did you reach?

_____

Reflection

(j) What are two things you liked about this activity?

• _____

• _____

(k) What did you find difficult about this activity?

_____

_____

(l) If you were to do this activity again, what would you do differently?

_____

_____

Self evaluation – The water and carbon cycles

Now that you have completed this chapter, how well do you feel you understand each of the following (tick the relevant column)?

Topic	🙂	😐	🙁
The stages of the water cycle			
Run-off			
Precipitation			
Transpiration			
The stages of the carbon cycle			
The biological process that takes place at each stage of the carbon cycle			
Fossil fuels			
Carbon sink			
Carbon source			
The organisms that contain carbon			

Action plan: What I need to do to improve my learning _____

_____

_____

ENERGY – OUR USE AND OUR NEED

Log onto **www.edcolearning.ie** to find the **Mind Map** for this chapter.

Homework questions

1 Name the fossil fuels.

_____

_____

_____

2 Explain the term 'non-renewable resources'.

_____

_____

3 Describe how fossil fuels are formed.

_____

_____

_____

_____

_____

4 Name three forms of renewable energy resources.

(i) _____

(ii) _____

(iii) _____

5 List three forms of energy that are used in your home. In your answer identify an appliance, within your home, that uses this form of energy.

(i) _____

(ii) _____

(iii) _____

6 List three advantages and three disadvantages of nuclear power:

(a) Advantages:

(i) _____

(ii) _____

(iii) _____

(b) Disadvantages:

(i) _____

(ii) _____

(iii) _____

7 Explain why the world's population requires new energy resources to be used.

_____

_____

_____

8 **Keywords.** Write one short sentence using each of the following words:

(a) Renewable _____

(b) Non-renewable _____

(c) Biomass _____

(d) Geothermal _____

(e) Solar _____

(f) Fossil fuel _____

(g) Nuclear power _____

Self evaluation – Energy – our use and our need

Now that you have completed this chapter, how well do you feel you understand each of the following (tick the relevant column)?

Topic	😀	😐	☹️
The three forms of energy			
Renewable forms of energy			
Non-renewable forms of energy			
Advantages and disadvantages of renewable and non-renewable forms of energy			
Fossil fuels			
The world's current energy needs			
The world's future energy needs			

Action plan: What I need to do to improve my learning _____

_____

Log onto **www.edcolearning.ie** to find the **Mind Map** for this chapter.

Homework questions

1   Explain the term 'climate change'.

_____

_____

2   Describe the term 'global warming'.

_____

_____

3   Explain the term 'greenhouse effect'.

_____

_____

4   Name the main greenhouse gases.

_____

_____

5   Describe how carbon dioxide is released naturally.

_____

_____

6   Explain the role of oceans in terms of global warming.

_____

_____

7   Outline the difference between cold and warm water in terms of absorption of carbon dioxide.

_____

_____

8 Describe the difference between lighter and darker objects in terms of sunlight.

_____

_____

9 Outline two effects of climate change.

(i) _____

(ii) _____

10 Explain the effects of the melting of the polar ice caps.

_____

_____

11 Describe any effects that Ireland, or your area within Ireland, is experiencing because of climate change.

_____

_____

12 Keywords. Write one short sentence using each of the following words:

(a) Climate change _____

(b) Global warming _____

(c) Greenhouse effect _____

(d) Greenhouse gases _____

(e) Reflected _____

(f) Absorb _____

(g) Glaciers _____

(h) Global dimming _____

(i) Carbon footprint _____

Activity 41.1: How can we demonstrate global warming?

(a) Date on which you carried out this activity _____

(b) In this activity what question did you ask yourself?

_____

(c) What predictions (hypothesis) did you make?

_____

_____

(d) How reliable and fair was your activity?

_____

_____

(e) What safety features did you consider and what did you do to reduce the risks?

_____

_____

(f) Identify controls in the activity.

_____

_____

(g) Identify any relevant dependent/independent/fixed variables in the activity.

_____

_____

(h) Record your results.

Table of results for one effervescent tablet

Time (minutes)	Temperature (°C)	Observations

Table of results for two effervescent tablets

Time (minutes)	Temperature (°C)	Observations

(i) Outline what this activity means to you in terms of global warming:

_____

_____

_____

_____

_____

Textbook question 41.7.

Research

(j) Monitor your energy use in your house over the period of a week.

Dates on which you carried out this activity: _____

Task	Mon	Tues	Weds	Thurs	Fri	Sat	Sun
Number of lights on in each room							
How many rooms have lights on when no person is in them							
Number of lights on in each room							
What electrical devices are on standby							
Temperature heating is set at							

Task	Mon	Tues	Weds	Thurs	Fri	Sat	Sun
Number of energy-saving bulbs in use							
Type of fuel used for heating							

Self evaluation – Climate change

Now that you have completed this chapter, how well do you feel you understand each of the following (tick the relevant column)?

Topic	:)	:|	:(
What the term 'climate change' means			
What the term 'global warming' means			
The greenhouse effect			
How the ocean plays its part in global warming			
Surface reflectivity			
Global dimming			
The effects of climate change			

Action plan: **What I need to do to improve my learning** _____

_____

_____

CHAPTER 42

SPACE EXPLORATION – 'TO INFINITY AND BEYOND!'

Log onto www.edcolearning.ie to find the **Mind Map** for this chapter.

Homework questions

1   Outline what the abbreviation 'NASA' stands for.

_____

2   Name Europe's space agency.

_____

3   Name the countries involved with Europe's space agency.

_____

_____

_____

4   List three examples of technology that were developed as a result of space exploration.

(i) _____

(ii) _____

(iii) _____

5   Name and explain a medical innovation that resulted from space exploration.

_____

_____

6   Outline three hazards to the human body that result from space exploration.

(i) _____

(ii) _____

(iii) _____

7   Describe any disaster that took place during a space mission.

_____

_____

_____

8 How do we know that gravity exists on Earth?

_____

_____

9 Give reasons why scientists are looking to Mars for future exploration.

_____

_____

10 Explore what you think would be the effect on Earth if there was micro/zero gravity.

_____

_____

11 **Keywords.** Write one short sentence using each of the following words:

(a) Exploration _____

(b) Technology _____

(c) Density _____

(d) Hazards _____

(e) Astronauts _____

Activity 42.2: How does being in space affect bone loss?

(a) Date on which you carried out this activity _____

(b) In this activity what question did you ask yourself?

_____

(c) What predictions (hypothesis) did you make?

_____

_____

(d) How reliable and fair was your activity?

_____

_____

(e) What safety features did you consider and what did you do to reduce the risks?

_____

_____

(f) Identify controls in the activity.

_____

_____

(g) Identify any relevant dependent/independent/fixed variables in the activity.

_____

_____

(h) Record your results.

Bag	Percentage of bone loss	Number of unbroken pieces of cereal	Observations
1 100%	0% Total number of pieces of puffed cereal in the bag =		
2 90%	10% Total number of pieces of puffed cereal in the bag =		
3 80%	20% Total number of pieces of puffed cereal in the bag =		
4 70%	30% Total number of pieces of puffed cereal in the bag =		
5 60%	40% Total number of pieces of puffed cereal in the bag =		

(i) What conclusion(s) did you reach?

_____

_____

Reflection

(j) What are two things you liked about this activity?

• _____

• _____

(k) What did you find difficult about this activity?

_____

_____

(l) If you were to do this activity again, what would you do differently?

_____

_____

Self evaluation – Space exploration – 'To infinity and beyond!'

Now that you have completed this chapter, how well do you feel you understand each of the following (tick the relevant column)?

Topic	🙂	😐	🙁
The benefits of space exploration			
Technologies that have resulted from space exploration			
Disasters that took place during space travel			
The effects of zero gravity on the human body			
The benefits of travelling to Mars			
Space exploration missions			

Action plan: What I need to do to improve my learning _____

_____

_____

Peer Assessment

Date:__/__/__

_____   _____   _____

Your name   Name of lab partner   Title of work

Success Criteria	How did this piece of work achieve the success criteria?

Two excellent points	This could be improved by...
1	
2	

Investigation Plan for Classroom-Based Assessment 1

| Student name: | Date: |
| | Class: |

Research question:

Equipment and materials request:

Proposed method:

| Approved by: | Date: |

CBA 1 (Extended Experimental Investigation) Template*

Date on which you carried out this investigation.

_____

In this investigation what question did you ask yourself?

_____

_____

What predictions (hypothesis) did you make?

_____

_____

_____

_____

How reliable and fair was your activity?_____

_____

Identify controls in the investigation.

_____

_____

Identify any relevant dependent/independent/fixed variables in the investigation.

Dependent: _____

Independent: _____

Fixed: _____

What safety features did you consider and what did you do to reduce the risks?

_____

_____

Equipment used in this investigation.

_____

_____

_____

What steps (procedure) did you follow?

_____

_____

_____

_____

_____

_____

* This is only a suggested template. Your report may be presented in a wide range of formats.

Draw a diagram of your apparatus.

Record your results in words and/or graphically.

What conclusion did you draw?

What went well in this investigation?

What did you find difficult about this investigation?

If you were to do this investigation again, what would you do differently?

CBA 2 (Science in Society Investigation) Template*

What topic did you choose?

_____

What was your research question?

_____

_____

Why did you choose this research question?

_____

_____

_____

_____

What sources did you use to research during your investigation?

_____

_____

_____

_____

_____

Were the sources you used reliable? Were any of the sources unreliable? How did you know these sources were reliable/unreliable?

_____

_____

_____

_____

_____

What did you learn from your investigation? What impact does your topic have on society and/or the environment? Did you present different sides of the argument?

_____

_____

_____

_____

_____

_____

_____

* This is only a suggested template. Your report may be presented in a wide range of formats.

_____

_____

_____

_____

_____

_____

_____

_____

_____

_____

What communication methods other than words (e.g. diagrams, photos, tables, graphs, charts and audio/visual recordings) did you use to present your information in your report? Why did you use these communication methods?

_____

_____

_____

_____

_____

_____

Do you think the knowledge you learned during your investigation was reliable? Explain your answer.

_____

_____

_____

_____

_____

_____

Features of Quality – CBA 1 (Extended Experimental Investigation)

The Features of Quality are the criteria used to assess your work as best fitting one of the four Descriptors below.

	Exceptional	Above Expectations	In Line with Expectations	Yet to Meet Expectations
Investigating	• Forms a testable hypothesis or prediction with justification • Describes considerations related to reliability and fairness • Outlines appropriate safety considerations, and describes the method used to accurately collect and record good-quality, reliable data in a manner that could be easily repeated. • Uses an innovative approach that truly enhances the work • Records a sufficient amount of good-quality data	• Forms a testable hypothesis or prediction with justification • Identifies the variable to be measured and the variable to be changed • Outlines appropriate safety considerations, and describes the method and equipment used to collect and record data • Records a sufficient amount of good-quality data	• With limited guidance, forms a testable hypothesis/prediction • Describes a safe method used to collect data – some of the steps are understandable but lack some detail • Records raw/primary data	• Uses a given investigation question • Is directed in using equipment to collect and record data • Data collection method described is not repeatable
Communicating	• Presents data in the most appropriate way using relevant scientific terminology and informative representations; calculations, if any, are performed to a high degree of accuracy • Describes the relationships between the variables	• Displays data neatly and accurately, using relevant scientific terminology and informative representations; calculations, if any, are performed to a high degree of accuracy • Describes the relationships between the variables	• Displays data on simple tables, charts or graphs, allowing for some errors in scaling or plotting • States a relationship between the variables	• Displays data on incomplete tables, charts or graphs, allowing for significant errors in scaling or plotting
Knowledge & Understanding	• Provides a justified conclusion supported by the data; identifies and explains any anomalous data • Uses relevant science knowledge to assess and describe whether the hypothesis has/has not been supported • Describes in detail the strengths and weaknesses of their own investigations, including appropriate improvements and/or refinements, or explains fully why no further improvements could reasonably be achieved	• Draws a conclusion consistent with the data and comments on whether the conclusion supports the hypothesis • Identifies the strengths and weaknesses of the investigation and suggests appropriate improvements, or explains why the procedures were of sufficient quality	• Draws a conclusion based on data collected, identifies some features of the investigation that could be improved and suggests improvements	• Comments on the investigation without making a conclusion/refinement to the investigation.

Features of Quality – CBA 2 (Science in Society Investigation)

The Features of Quality are the criteria used to assess your work as best fitting one of the four Descriptors below.

	Exceptional	Above Expectations	In Line with Expectations	Yet to Meet Expectations
Investigating	• Chooses an interesting or novel topic and research question • Finds information about the topic from a large number of varied and balanced sources, and gives a complete reference list • Evaluates the reliability (relevance, accuracy and bias) of the sources	• Chooses an interesting or novel topic and research question • Finds information about the topic from a number of balanced sources, and gives a complete reference list • Considers the reliability and quality (relevance, accuracy and bias) of the sources	• Chooses a topic and research question with some teacher guidance • Finds some useful sources of information about the topic and gives some references • Gives some consideration to the reliability or quality (relevance, accuracy and bias) of the sources	• Chooses a topic but is given the research question • Is directed to sources of information about the topic • Uses very few sources with little evidence of what the sources are
Communicating	• Clearly positions the topic as science in society; explains the relevant science and the impact of the topic on society and/or the environment • Presents the investigation in a very well-structured way (that is clear and easy to read) using relevant scientific terminology and informative representations; uses an innovative approach that truly enhances the work • Explains different sides of the argument in detail	• Positions the topic as science in society; explains the relevant science and the impact of the topic on society and/or the environment • Presents the investigation in a well-structured way (that is clear and easy to read), using relevant scientific terminology and informative representations • Considers information from different sides of the argument	• Mentions in passing the impact of the topic on society and/or the environment. • Presents the investigation in a structured way using relevant scientific terminology • Provides information on different sides of the argument	• Presents the investigation using some scientific terminology • Presents the investigation in a way that is somewhat structured
Knowledge & Understanding	• Views on the chosen topic are considered and discussed in depth • Gives a justified personal opinion informed by research, linking the information to the argument and using science explanations	• Gives a personal opinion informed by research linking the information to the argument and using science explanations	• Gives a personal opinion informed by research with some explanation	• Gives a personal opinion without explanation or a link to the original question

Notes

Notes